STRAYHORN

AN ILLUSTRATED LIFE

STRAYHORN
AN ILLUSTRATED LIFE

PRODUCED BY Billy Strayhorn Songs, Inc.

CONTRIBUTIONS BY David Hajdu, Walter van de Leur, Robert Levi, Bruce Mayhall Rastrelli, AND Gregory A. Morris

EDITED BY A. Alyce Claerbaut AND David Schlesinger

BOLDEN
AN AGATE IMPRINT
CHICAGO

Printed in China

Library of Congress Cataloging-in-Publication Data

Strayhorn : an illustrated life / edited by A. Alyce Claerbaut and David Schlesinger.
    pages cm
 Includes bibliographical references and index.
 ISBN 978-1-932841-98-5 (hardback) -- ISBN 1-932841-98-9 (hard cover) -- ISBN 978-1-57284-765-1 (ebook)
 1. Strayhorn, Billy. 2. Composers--United States--Biography. 3. Jazz musicians--United States--Biography. 4. Strayhorn, Billy--Pictorial works. 5. Composers--United States--Biography--Pictorial works. 6. Jazz musicians--United States--Biography--Pictorial works. I. Claerbaut, A. Alyce, editor. II. Schlesinger, David, 1984- editor.
 ML410.S9325S77 2015
 781.65092--dc23
 [B]
                              2015021651

10 9 8 7 6 5 4 3 2 1   15 16 17 18

Bolden is an imprint of Agate Publishing. Agate books are available in bulk at discount prices. For more information, go to agatepublishing.com.

In memory of Lillian Young Strayhorn,
whose persistent maternal love and nurture of Baby Boy Strayhorn
gave the world an unspeakable gift.

Ever up and onward!
—Billy Strayhorn

CONTENTS

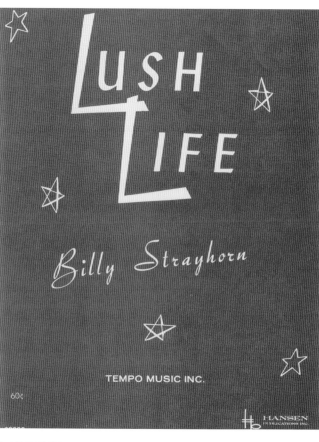

FOREWORD

BY RAMSEY LEWIS

AMERICAN JAZZ COMPOSER, PIANIST, RECORDING ARTIST, AND RADIO PERSONALITY

The name Billy Strayhorn (1915–1967) should be known to anyone who claims to be knowledgeable of the major music shapers of the twentieth century. As a musician, I have always been aware of his name and reputation as a pianist, arranger, and composer because—despite the fact that he is not a household name to the general public—he is highly revered by musicians and industry insiders worldwide. On the occasion of his centennial, there are celebrations of his legacy throughout the United States and abroad.

Strayhorn's immense talent was noted in 1938 by Duke Ellington who was already famous and established in history as a great composer and bandleader. He was so impressed with Strayhorn that their first meeting launched a collaborative musical partnership lasting nearly three decades. Ellington came to refer to Strayhorn as his "writing and arranging companion." He further declared that Strayhorn was "my right arm, my left arm, all the eyes in the back of my head, my brainwaves in his head, and his in mine." Their musical collaboration is historically intertwined. Together they forged some of the most creative repertoire of

the jazz orchestra. Strayhorn vested himself in the Ellington style so completely that many musicians were not able to determine who actually wrote what.

Yet, recent research on Strayhorn has revealed that he was a composer of singular genius and had a distinctive musical voice from the beginning. His highly acclaimed composition "Lush Life" was written in his pre-Ellington days during his high school years. Although it never became part of the Ellington book—it was never recorded or performed by Ellington—it still emerged as one of the top torch songs of all time. Strayhorn also wrote the undisputed first jazz musical (ca. 1935) shortly after graduating from high school. *Fantastic Rhythm* was professionally produced for two years in western Pennsylvania. Three songs made it into the Ellington book, "Something to Live For," "My Little Brown Book," and "Your Love Has Faded."

Even though I have performed Strayhorn's music during my career, *Strayhorn: An Illustrated Life* is enriching my understanding of him both as a great American composer and as a fellow human being. *Strayhorn* is a collection of writings, interviews, and annotated photos that reveal this American master by depicting people he knew, places he frequented, his style of dress, his family and friends, his work with the band, and the vastness and diversity of his artistic accomplishments both within and beyond the Ellington orbit. His involvement in the civil rights movement is

a feature of *Strayhorn* that reveals even more about the man himself and of the "four freedoms," cited by Ellington, by which he lived:

1. Freedom from hate, unconditionally,
2. Freedom from self-pity,
3. Freedom from the fear of possibly doing something that may help someone else more than it would you, and
4. Freedom from the kind of pride that could make a man feel that he is better than his brother.

The story of Billy Strayhorn is compelling and is of interest to readers of all backgrounds. We have as much to enjoy from the music Billy made as we have to learn from the way he lived his life.

INTRODUCTION

Billy Strayhorn spent many years as an unsung hero, even though his music was one of the major forces in the shaping of the jazz canon. Strayhorn's enormous contributions to the American songbook and the jazz repertory orchestra have been historically underrated and neglected. The short, incomplete story of Strayhorn's career is that he collaborated for three decades as the "writing and arranging companion" of Duke Ellington. But that doesn't begin to describe Strayhorn's remarkable contributions to music nor the inspiring and fascinating story of his life.

This book and all the efforts of Billy Strayhorn Songs, Inc., the organization formed to bring recognition to Billy Strayhorn after his death, aim to tell and illustrate the story of a life that is as compelling as his music.

Today—one hundred years after Strayhorn's birth—is a new and exciting time for Billy Strayhorn and the people who have come to appreciate his music and spirit. His songs have been performed by literally hundreds of great artists, including Rosemary Clooney, Ella Fitzgerald, Sarah Vaughan, Marian McPartland, Natalie Cole, Linda Rondstadt, Donna Summer, Dizzy Gillespie, Nat King Cole, classical orchestras, wind and brass ensembles both jazz and classical, and theatrical and Tin Pan Alley settings among others, and the list goes on and on. His torch ballad "Lush Life" was recorded by pop star Lady Gaga as a solo on *Cheek to Cheek*, a collaborative album with jazz great Tony Bennett. Today there is a new generation of artists performing his works in recordings, on television, in film, and on the stage.

Strayhorn's road to his calling as a musician had many obstacles that still impact his legacy. He grew up in twentieth-century America and faced many challenges. He was a black prodigy of classical music who was advised by teachers and other influential adults that he would not be able to pursue a career in that particular field because of his race. He was often in orchestras where he was the sole African American. He had a trio during his post high school years that featured an integrated group, and he couldn't even stay in the same places as other members of his group. He was also gay and he practiced his lifestyle openly, which in his age was not tolerated, and those who did suffered many consequences.

Strayhorn, however, unfailingly overcame these obstacles and lived his life freely. And what's more, he did so with grace, style, and a breathtaking creative output. Upon receiving the Medal of Freedom from President Nixon in 1969, Duke Ellington described Strayhorn's commitment to various kinds of freedom.

> This is the Presidential Medal of Freedom. And the word "freedom" is one, coincidentally, that we are using at the moment in our sacred concert.
>
> And, of course, we speak of freedom of expression and we speak of freedom generally as being something very sweet and fat and things like that. In the end when we get down to the payoff, what we actually say is that we would like very much to mention the four major freedoms that my friend and writing-and-arranging composer, Billy Strayhorn, lived by and enjoyed.
>
> That was freedom from hate, unconditionally; freedom from self-pity; freedom from fear of possibly doing something that may help someone else more than it would him; and freedom from the kind of pride that could make a man feel that he is better than his brother.

In short, Billy Strayhorn's moral freedoms are those that emanate from the heart. They lead to the external freedoms for which Martin Luther King Jr. strove. Strayhorn was counted among King's friends and confidants during the civil rights movement.

The other major reason the Strayhorn legacy has been historically underrated is due to the fact that he became obscured in the shadow of his boss, the great Duke Ellington, who at the time was already one of the greatest musicians of all time. Strayhorn often went uncredited and under credited for work he did. After his death in 1967 his music all but disappeared. At that time, Gregory Morris, Strayhorn's nephew, became the executor of Strayhorn's estate. He cleared out his residence after his death and came upon boxes of written music that were part of Strayhorn's final holdings. This material appeared to be a disorganized and chaotic collection hastily packed in moving boxes, large mailing envelopes, and bankers' file storage boxes. A year after Strayhorn's death, it was evident that the documented record of Strayhorn's written work was grossly incomplete and underestimated. Those boxes of papers turned out to contain approximately eight thousand pages of manuscripts and notes that were to unlock the treasures of the Strayhorn legacy thirty years later.

When Ellington died in 1974, there were major movements to preserve and expand his legacy, particularly in the '90s, looking forward to the 1999 Ellington centennial. In the quest to mount a campaign making him the singularly most important composer of the twentieth century, promotion practices diminished Strayhorn's role. Compact disc covers of reissued Ellington recordings that once bore Strayhorn's photo were redesigned to include only Ellington's. Strayhorn's name was in effect erased in the listing of credits for programs, and he was minimized in articles about Ellington. It's not that Ellington didn't

November 29, 1915 **William Thomas Strayhorn born in Miami Valley Hospital, Dayton, Ohio, to James Strayhorn and the former Lillian Young.**

1926 **Billy Strayhorn begins private lessons.**

1915   1920   1925   1930

1920 **After periods of living in various locations including Montclair, New Jersey, the Strayhorns settle in greater Pittsburgh, Pennsylvania.**

1927 **In seventh grade, Strayhorn starts his music study at Westinghouse High School under Carl McVicker and other teachers.**

deserve this recognition—he did. It's that Strayhorn deserved better than he received.

But there were other things that happened as well. In 1993, the Ellington family decided to no longer run Tempo Music, the publishing company that Ellington established in the 1940s. It was sold to a major publisher. Strayhorn's obscurity continued, and in 1997, the Strayhorn family decided to take advantage of a clause in the copyright law that allowed original authors or their heirs to terminate former publishers and recapture publishing rights. This clause was reinforced in 1998 with the passing of the Sonny Bono Copyright Term Extension Act. After intense litigation

instituted by the Ellington publishers, the Strayhorns prevailed and were able to do the business of publishing the Strayhorn catalog with a copublisher that they engaged to handle the administrative work for this effort.

Beginning in the mid-'90s, the interest in Billy Strayhorn and his work has been growing. The explosion in interest was sparked by the 1996 biography, *Lush Life*, by David Hajdu. In March 1997, a certificate of incorporation was granted to the heirs of the estate of Billy Strayhorn and a small family corporation known officially as Billy Strayhorn Songs, Inc. (BSSI) was born. This step was a major milestone and a

September 1936
Strayhorn attends
the Pittsburgh
Musical Institute,
a private music
conservatory.

1930

1935

1929–1933 While at Westinghouse, Strayhorn engages in various musical activities, including participation in the Orchestra Club. As first pianist with the Senior Orchestra, Strayhorn performs Edvard Grieg's *Piano Concerto, opus 16*, among other pieces. During this period, he begins composing his first works combining jazz and classical elements.

1933–1936 Working on the piece sporadically over a period of several years, Strayhorn composes "Lush Life."

November 6, 1935 Premiere of *Fantastic Rhythm*, a musical revue with book, music, and lyrics by Billy Strayhorn, performed at Westinghouse High School.

long way from the spring day in 1965 when Strayhorn asked his nephew Gregory Morris to handle his business affairs in the event of his death. Since 1997 the family has formalized a means of working together as a unit to capture, manage, preserve, and expand the legacy of Billy Strayhorn.

Also in the '90s, musicologist Walter van de Leur published a scholarly treatise titled "Something to Live For." Van de Leur's work added considerably to the scholarship surrounding the contributions of Billy Strayhorn to the Ellington catalogue and to a deeper understanding of Strayhorn's genius.

While immersed in the music of Billy Strayhorn, Van de Leur continued documenting what Billy

Strayhorn had written. His examination and study led to the copyrighting of some seventy-seven new compositions and suites for the heirs of Billy Strayhorn and BSSI. Furthermore, Van de Leur completed a dissertation in which he documented additional compositions and suites that Strayhorn had a hand in arranging and composing. Since the inception of BSSI, seventy-seven solely Strayhorn titles have been added to his body of work as a result of both post-litigation catalog assessment and Walter van de Leur's research.

Van de Leur's dissertation was published by Oxford University Press in 2002 under the title *Something to Live For: The Music of Billy Strayhorn*. Most importantly, appendices A–D of that work provide a

1941 During a radio ban on music composed by members of the ASCAP, including Duke Ellington, Strayhorn emerges through compositions including "Take the 'A' Train," "Johnny Come Lately," "Chelsea Bridge," and "After All."

1937–1938 Strayhorn performs around the Pittsburgh area with his own jazz combo, The Mad Hatters.

December 2, 1938 Billy Strayhorn meets Duke Ellington at the Stanley Theater, where Ellington was performing with his orchestra.

January 23, 1939 Strayhorn visits Ellington at the Adams Theater in Newark, New Jersey, and accepts Ellington's offer to serve as Ellington's collaborator. Shortly after this, Strayhorn moves from Pittsburgh into Ellington's home at 409 Edgecombe Avenue in Harlem's Sugar Hill District.

March 21, 1939 The Duke Ellington Orchestra records its first Strayhorn composition, "Something to Live For."

1940

comprehensive listing of Strayhorn's recordings and compositions. As a result of Van de Leur's efforts, more than four hundred compositions have been credited to Strayhorn's corpus of work to date.

As momentum around Strayhorn's story continued to grow, filmmaker Robert Levi developed a documentary about Strayhorn. He had already directed a 1991 documentary film about the Duke called *Duke Ellington: Reminiscing in Tempo*. However, he felt that the new revelations about Strayhorn required him to finish his work represented in that film. BSSI commissioned him to produce *Billy Strayhorn: Lush Life*, which aired on the Public Broadcasting Service (PBS) in 2007.

Even more recently, new recordings of Strayhorn's music are being released. Aside from countless musicians interpreting Strayhorn's work, two specific watershed releases have gone a long way in making the breadth of Strayhorn's music known. Walter van de Leur and the Dutch Jazz Orchestra recorded a four-CD box set of Strayhorn's music. Walter provided the research, performance editions, and the liner notes for this production. And in 2014 Storyville Records, a subsidiary of Music Sales, distributed a seven-disc set of historic recordings of Strayhorn compositions made throughout the years by jazz giants. Beginning in the 1990s there has been a steady surge in the number of albums made in

December 1946
Strayhorn wins
DownBeat readers
poll for arranger.

May 8, 1956 National television broadcasts of
Ellington-Strayhorn theatrical collaboration *A
Drum Is a Woman*, an allegorical history of
jazz told in music and dance.

1945

1950

1955

March 29, 1949
First recording
of "Lush Life" by
Nat King Cole.

1950 Strayhorn joins the Copasetics, a fraternal organization
of show-business insiders based in Harlem. Soon he is elected
president and leads the group in social and charitable activities.

November 1950 Ellington-Strayhorn piano duet recorded,
released on LP billed as the Billy Strayhorn Trio.

tribute to Strayhorn by both established and emerging musicians. Many of the new artists represent a diverse palette of interpretations including Latin, post bop, experimental, traditional, and hip-hop.

Today is a new and exciting day for Billy Strayhorn, and we are the privileged ones who are sharing the joy of his work and legacy.

BOOK FEATURES

A man with the creative intellect and deep soul that Strayhorn had leaves his mark on the world. The best way to remember Strayhorn's life and what he accomplished is to consider what he left behind: the songs he wrote and the memories he left with the

people in his life. This book attempts to bring some of these songs and stories to a wide audience through biographical history, personal memoir, critical appreciation, and images relating to different eras and parts of Strayhorn's life and career.

MAIN PARTS

Part One: Musical Orbits is written by A. Alyce Claerbaut and traces the arc of Strayhorn's musical career. Claerbaut is Strayhorn's niece and the current president of BSSI. Her writing is an amalgamation of family stories and remembered conversations with Strayhorn himself, informed by the works of Hajdu, Levi, and Van de Leur as well as tête-à-têtes with jazz aficionados in her capacity as a producer of jazz programs and her involvement with jazz education. Alyce has been discovering and rediscovering Billy Strayhorn through many voices for most of her adult life, and this part of the book brings together her discoverings.

Part Two: Moral Freedoms is told by Strayhorn scholar and choral conductor and performer Bruce Mayhall Rastrelli, who discusses Strayhorn's involvement with the civil rights movement of the 1960s and the ways in which his sexuality did and did not influence his music and career.

In addition to the main story told in each of the two parts of this book, there are some recurring features.

PERSPECTIVES

In writing *Lush Life*, David Hajdu interviewed untold numbers of family members, friends, and musicians who knew and worked with Strayhorn. Many of the stories he learned are told in his narrative biography, but the Perspectives feature in this book recounts previously untold narratives by ten of Strayhorn's intimates and collaborators. The warmth of Strayhorn's character and the vastness of his imagination come across in these personal remembrances.

In Hajdu's own explanation,

> Billy Strayhorn may have been the best-known little-known figure in American culture. Although his name was not widely recognized during his lifetime, he was well known to countless musicians, dancers, actors, writers, painters, filmmakers, choreographers, civic leaders, and political activists, as well as innumerable uncelebrated people whom he regarded with respect and affection. Strayhorn had an audience with Queen Elizabeth II, and worked with the Rev. Martin Luther King Jr. His closest confidante was Lena Horne, and one

of his dearest friends was an elevator operator. "Billy loved everybody," Lena Horne told me in an interview for my book, *Lush Life: A Biography of Billy Strayhorn* (1996). "And everybody loved Billy— almost everybody."

Throughout his life and after his death, Strayhorn's friends, creative collaborators, and associates held dear their memories of a man who never seemed to care much for attention. Here is a selection of those memories, as they were recounted in interviews I conducted between 1984 and 1995.

Interviews that Hajdu conducted with the following people are featured throughout the book: **Lillian Strayhorn Dicks**, sister; **Ruth Ellington Boatwright**, Duke Ellington's sister; **Aaron Bridgers**, pianist, friend, and partner; **Herb Jeffries**, singer in the Duke Ellington Orchestra; **Lena Horne**, friend, singer, actor, and activist; **Honi Coles**, dancer and member of the Copasetics; **Marian McPartland**, pianist and broadcaster; **Donald Shirley**, pianist; **Rosemary Clooney**, singer; **Jimmy Woode**, bassist in the Duke Ellington Orchestra.

VIGNETTES

Robert Levi also sat down with Strayhorn's closest collaborators and loved ones when creating his award-winning documentary film *Billy Strayhorn: Lush Life* for *Independent Lens* on PBS. Levi's film captures rare film footage of Strayhorn playing, as well as engrossing interviews with people who knew Strayhorn and his music well. Not all of his research and interviews made it into his film, however, and this book presents the choice selections from what was left on the cutting room floor. These Vignettes present various people in Strayhorn's life sharing their memories about specific stories from and characteristics of Strayhorn's life.

Mid- to late 1950s Strayhorn records
extensively with Johnny Hodges, serving as
musical director, arranger, and pianist.

December 1961 Billy Strayhorn and the Orchestra LP
recorded for release on the Verve label.

April 14, 1959 Billy Strayhorn
Septet LP recorded.

December 19–21, 1966
Ellington-Strayhorn
collaboration *The Far
East Suite* recorded.

January 1961 Strayhorn solo LP, *The Peaceful Side*, recorded in
Paris for release by United Artists Records.

1960

1965

April 28, 1957 Debut
of Ellington-Strayhorn
collaboration *Such Sweet
Thunder*, an instrumental
suite inspired by the works
of Shakespeare, at New
York's Town Hall.

June 1960
Ellington-Strayhorn
adaptation of *The
Nutcracker Suite*
recorded.

May the new year
be as good to you
as you were kind
to me during my illness

Billy Strayhorn

May 31, 1967 Billy
Strayhorn dies
of cancer of the
esophagus at
age fifty-one.

In Levi's words,

Billy Strayhorn: Lush Life is a film that tells the story of a gifted composer whose twenty-nine year collaboration with his co-writer, Duke Ellington, produced a body of work without rival in originality and range. Yet, while Ellington is considered by many experts to be the most influential composer in jazz history, Billy Strayhorn's contributions are too frequently overlooked and undervalued.

Making a film about a prolific yet unfailingly modest genius was a challenge. Numerous scenes in the documentary were radically trimmed, others were omitted, and, as always in filmmaking,

important source material wound up on the "cutting room floor." Here are some of our favorite stories, as well as insights from new interviews that we're pleased to share. As Strayhorn's award-winning biographer David Hajdu noted on camera: "Billy Strayhorn is of enormous historical importance for a dozen reasons that have nothing to do with Duke Ellington. Yes, Ellington and his orchestra performed a great deal of music that Billy Strayhorn composed, but there's a whole lot more to Strayhorn than Duke Ellington."

In addition to some of the figures in BSSI as well as some of the people Hajdu interviewed, Levi's Vignettes feature takes from **Fred Hersch**, pianist, bandleader, and composer; **Herb Jordan**, writer and composer; **Bill Charlap**, pianist and bandleader; **Terell Stafford**, trumpeter, bandleader, and composer; **Luther Henderson**, composer, arranger, and orchestrator; **Jean Bach**, colleague and publicist; **Gerald Wilson**, composer, bandleader, and trumpeter; **David Baker**, composer and bandleader; **Mercedes Ellington**, granddaughter of Duke Ellington; **Billy Taylor**, pianist and bandleader; **Clark Terry**, trumpeter and bandleader; **Dianne Reeves**, jazz vocalist; **Chico Hamilton**, drummer and bandleader; **Tammy McCann**, jazz vocalist; **Nancy Wilson**, jazz vocalist; **Gail Lumet Buckley**, author; **Jon Hendricks**, jazz vocalist and lyricist.

LINER NOTES

The Liner Notes sections in this book are written by Walter van de Leur, author of the definitive book about Strayhorn's music. The Liner Notes feature covers a few scores of Strayhorn's most famous and most notable tunes, discussing why they matter and what to listen for. In addition to these critical appreciations, Van de Leur has provided a recommended recording for each song. Specific recordings are a

matter of personal taste, as Van de Leur notes, but he tried to highlight artists who pioneered Strayhorn's work. These aren't the definitive recordings, but they are beautiful and moving realizations of some of Strayhorn's best songs and a great place to start or deepen your appreciation of Strayhorn's music.

MUSIC SCORES

The music scores presented in this volume were written by Billy Strayhorn. In addition to his having composed the music, these are his manuscripts—penned by his own hand and recovered from file cabinets in his residence after he died. The music scores presented are partial, in most cases showing only the first page of a tune, and do not reflect definitive versions of any one song. Indeed they come from various stages of Strayhorn's career—early and late—and may be from arrangements made for solo recordings or concerts, small combos, specific singers or bands, or Ellington's jazz orchestra. For a full account of the manuscripts recovered from Strayhorn's belongings, as well as their historical and musicological significance, consult Van de Leur's *Something to Live For: The Music of Billy Strayhorn*.

MUSICAL ORBITS

The musical orbits that Billy Strayhorn traveled in were diverse and large. He composed brilliant songs for the best big band in the country and was equally adept at arranging pieces or providing accompaniment for unique voices. He was a pioneer of jazz musical theater, a brilliant combo composer and artist, a second-to-none lyricist, and a serious student of classical music. To understand Billy Strayhorn's musical legacy, you have to understand the overlapping orbits of his life and career.

Billy was born to Lillian and James Strayhorn in the city of Dayton, Ohio. The year was 1915 in the month of November. He was a sickly child who was referred to as "Baby Boy" Strayhorn. Having already lost two young children after the birth of the eldest Strayhorn child, James, perhaps his parents were wary about giving a name to another child who could have slipped away from them; they waited to file a legal name for him until five years later in Pittsburgh, Pennsylvania. Remarkably, upon arriving on the Pittsburgh scene, this young family had already lived in four states. This was not exactly the most stable environment for the raising of young children and amid this instability, it may have been that only his mother, Lillian, saw that spark of genius peeking out of the glistening eyes of the youngster who was to become one of the greatest composers of the century.

Billy's father became very embittered by the various dead-end jobs that seemed plentiful in his case. It was fertile ground for the creation of a drinker. And drink he did, often taking out his frustrations on his family. Billy was small and quiet, consequently becoming an easy target for his dad's wrath. On one occasion Billy laid his glasses on the floor while reading a book. His father entered the room and deliberately crushed them and left the room laughing.[1]

EARLY YEARS

Lillian Young Strayhorn attended Shaw University in North Carolina, which was one of the first historically black colleges in the United States and was founded immediately after the Civil War. Lillian was a lady of refinement and grace with high hopes for a good life. Her husband, James Strayhorn, was a man feeling the pressures of discrimination that kept his hopes unfulfilled. His embitterment contributed to an abusive household. Billy was the most vulnerable of their children, and

Miami Valley Hospital, Dayton, Ohio, birth certificate of "Baby Boy" Strayhorn, 4:15 a.m., November 29, 1915. Billy wasn't legally named until several years later.

Billy and his "satin doll," his mother, Lillian Young Strayhorn, at an early 1950s family reunion in Pittsburgh. He brought her fancy gifts whenever he came home. "She's the only reason he came home," said his sister Lillian. When he was there, "Mama was in her glory."

Billy credited his grandmother Lizzie Craig Strayhorn as his earliest musical influence. This photograph was made in front of Lizzie Strayhorn's house in North Carolina just after her death. (She died from cancer on June 19, 1923.) Sister Georgia poses with seven-year-old James and infant brother Johnny.

The women in Billy's family: sister Lillian Strayhorn Dicks (1930–2005), mother Lillian Young Strayhorn (1892–1966), and sister Georgia Strayhorn Morris Conaway (1921–1974).

his mother became his protector from a father given to an ill temper and violence. Lillian saw to it that Billy had the chance to visit his grandparents in Hillsborough, North Carolina, during the summers between the ages of five and eleven. This period was a fertile time in Billy's emotional and artistic development. His grandmother was a church pianist. Billy began exploring the piano and picking out tunes that were played at church. This love of the piano and music continued even after his return to Pittsburgh. His love of the piano became the core of his development as a musician.

The importance of the piano was such that during his teen years he began selling papers and working

Graduation photo from Westinghouse High School, Pittsburgh. There were two graduating classes each year; Billy's was the January 1934 cohort.

"MY LITTLE BROWN BOOK" (CA. 1935)

In the winter of 1935, Strayhorn's former schoolmates at Westinghouse High in Pittsburgh asked him to help them out with their act for "Stunt Day"—a yearly event for which the graduating class organized a vaudeville program with music and comedy. Word of Strayhorn's musical proficiency was spreading in the Pittsburgh area. While delivering goods for Pennfield Pharmacy, Strayhorn often ended up on a piano bench. "When I would deliver packages, people would ask me to 'sit down and play us one of your songs,'" he later reminisced. For his alma mater, he ended up writing a twenty-minute Gershwinesque musical show, which he titled *Fantastic Rhythm*. After a successful premiere, Strayhorn reworked it into a full-scale musical production. Accompanied by the Moonlight Harbor Band, a popular dance band in Pittsburgh's black ballrooms, the show toured the greater Pittsburgh area in 1935 and thereafter went on the road in western Pennsylvania. Most of the music is lost, with the exception of "My Little Brown Book," a beautiful, romantic song. Strayhorn arranged the piece a number of times for the Ellington orchestra, alternately featuring singers Herb Jeffries and Al Hibbler, who performed it many times in the 1940s.

—*Walter van de Leur*

RECOMMENDED RECORDING

○ Aretha Franklin, *The Great American Songbook* (1963; Columbia 2011)

This image of Billy was forever emblazoned in the memory of jazz aficionados when it appeared as the cover photo for the paperback edition (1997) of David Hajdu's *Lush Life: A Biography of Billy Strayhorn*.

"SMADA" (CA. 1935)

"Smada," apparently dedicated to the black Los Angeles disc jockey Joe Adams, was first recorded in 1951, but the piece is much older. Well before he met Ellington, Strayhorn had already written two versions of "Smada," and over the course of the 1940s, more followed. The oldest known title is "Ugly Ducklin'"—an earlier title, "Smoky City" (Pittsburgh?), was crossed out. It may have been played by one of the local bands that Strayhorn wrote for, such as the Moonlight Harbor Band, the twelve-piece outfit that accompanied the commercial edition of *Fantastic Rhythm*. Strayhorn registered the piece for copyright as "Jennie Lou Stomp" in 1944. Tempo Music reregistered it as "Smada" in 1951, with Ellington's name added, even though the latter had nothing to do with the work. The title found in most versions, however, is "Don't Take My Love," which suggests that Strayhorn wrote the lyrics to it. The line "please, don't take my love," perfectly fits the opening phrase.

Given the utterly hip chord changes, the composition date of the work is remarkable. The A-sections of "Smada" circle around a repeated two-chord structure, a concept that points to the so-called modal jazz pieces of Miles Davis, Gil Evans, and John Coltrane in the late 1950s. Strayhorn worked with these ideas more than twenty years before they became fashionable in jazz.

—Walter van de Leur

RECOMMENDED RECORDING

○ Michael Hashim Quartet, *Lotus Blossom* (Stash Records)

---

other jobs to save money until he could buy his own piano because his parents did not have the means to provide one for him. The upright player piano with a broken roll that he purchased became the symbol of a great career that was to be.

THE EMERGENCE OF A VIRTUOSO

Over the next several years, Strayhorn made great strides in his musical development, composing songs and developing skills that would serve him throughout his career. At Westinghouse High School, he studied under Carl McVicker, a wonderful trumpet player and director of the band and orchestra. It was during this period that Billy wrote a number of works. Two were classical pieces: a piano waltz titled "Valse" and "Concerto for Piano and Percussion." The latter composition was performed at the 1934 commencement ceremony at Westinghouse.

After graduation, Strayhorn entered a rich creative period. Between the ages of eighteen and twenty-two he made significant accomplishments as a composer. One year out of high school, Billy returned to his roots at Westinghouse and helped to plan a musical revue. He composed ten original songs providing both music and lyrics for the show titled *Fantastic Rhythm*. "My Little Brown Book" is a song from the show that was later recorded by the Duke Ellington band. The show was produced in western Pennsylvania and in Virginia for two years (the illustrations on the following pages reveal just how developed the production was).

Manuscript in pencil of the Gershwinesque opening of Billy's 1935 theater piece, *Fantastic Rhythm*. Its title was clearly intended to convey the artistic influence of a composer at the peak of his career on the young, aspiring Strayhorn. Under-classmate Oliver Fowler heard the twenty-minute piece at Westinghouse High School and convinced Billy to compose a total of ten songs for an expanded version.

Oliver "Boggie" Fowler, organizer and producer, was also master of ceremonies and in some performances directed "Smiling Billy" Alston and his Moonlight Harbor Band.

ABOVE, FROM LEFT: After 1,200 attended the first performances and the *Courier* called it a "howling success," Fowler secured financial backing from Al Wess and Jess Williams and booked performances at Schenley, Baxter, and Allderdice high schools. In 1936 it played at the prestigious Roosevelt Theater in Pittsburgh and through 1938 at major black theaters in Rankin, Braddock, Homestead, East Liberty, and Orangetown—all without Billy. "He made it known that he intended to do greater things," Ralph Koger said. § Costumer Dorothy Ford (left) and female lead Marie Pleasant. To Billy's accompaniment she was the first to sing "My Little Brown Book" (later an Ellington/Al Hibbler hit), and she arranged and led several of the choral numbers.

Cassie Birch and Harriett Cralle were among the dance teams choreographed by professional tap dancer Harold Belcher. Christine Thomas cocreated the routines. Posters emphasized the fifty beautiful girls; the show also utilized twenty-five tuxedoed, handsome men.

Clyde Broadus, "sensational tap dancer and side-splitting comedian, who has appeared in shows throughout Pennsylvania, Ohio and New York States" and "long acclaimed by the ofay clubs as Pittsburgh's own 'Bojangles'" (*Pittsburgh Courier*), was stunned by Billy's brilliance. "He'd create a song out of *nothing* . . . he'd just sit down there—dit, dit, dit, dit— right there. I asked him 'How do you do that?' He said, 'I don't know. It just comes to me.'"

Spartan outdoor venue for one of the southwestern Pennsylvania runs of *Fantastic Rhythm*. Boggie Fowler said, "See, back in them days, you couldn't go but certain different theaters, because they didn't allow colored. So we went to all the colored theaters—we'd go to all the colored places that you could go."

Over time the cast changed somewhat—mostly to provide professional performers for high-profile venues. The second group of "Sob Sisters" was more adept than the first. Dorothy Ford, from the first group, said, "I couldn't sing what Billy originally wrote. So he changed it to something I could just practically talk." Billy Eckstine and Erroll Garner brought their artistry to later performances. § Newspaper ad for the Schenley High School performances of December 1935. All three Pittsburgh papers covered the production. § Cast of the 1937 troupe. In written notes, Fowler claims writing credit and points out Dolores Gomez, his "old sweets" whose "Harlem Rumba" was "particularly beautiful," according to the *Courier*.

Just II Weeks More

16 NEW SONG HITS

50 BEAUTIFUL, SHAPELY GIRLS

★ ★ ★ FOR ★ ★ ★

"Fantastic Rhythm"

WILL MAKE ITS LAST DEBUT OF

1935

Schenley High School Auditorium

During the 3rd Week of December

An Oliver Fowler Production

"SO THIS IS LOVE" (CA. 1935)

When interviewed, Strayhorn tended to downplay the musical life he led in Pittsburgh prior to joining the Ellington entourage. He told jazz writer Stanley Dance that he had written "a couple of things," when, in fact, he had composed and arranged relentlessly for nearly a decade. Of all his teenage work, only a handful of pieces became known to a wider audience: "Something to Live For," "Your Love Has Faded," "My Little Brown Book," "Smada," and "Lush Life."

One of the most remarkable scores that turned up among his private manuscripts is "So This Is Love," written around the time when he must have been working on its famous twin, "Lush Life." "So This Is Love" may not be as convincing lyrically, but the musical setting is nevertheless equally brilliant. The song convincingly expresses the dazzling feelings that come with a budding affair. Strayhorn's music provides an emotional counterpoint to his lyrics (such as the melodic drop on "love" over a highly unstable chord: love is unsure) to voice the uncertainties of young romance.

—Walter van de Leur

RECOMMENDED RECORDINGS

○ Dutch Jazz Orchestra, *Something to Live For: The Music of Billy Strayhorn* (Challenge 2002)

○ Dianne Reeves, *Lush Life* (Blue Note 2007)

A GIFT FOR COLLABORATION

Strayhorn honed his musical leadership skills during this time. His ability to work tactfully and sensitively with a range of people allowed him to collaborate with a diverse set of musicians and artists and to build long-lasting and intimate friendships throughout his entire life. During this time, he developed a cadre of local young musicians, some whom he knew from high school, from which he drew for small group ensembles.

The Mad Hatters was one such trio for which he developed a band book that included "Something to Live For" and "Your Love Has Faded." The Mad Hatters were racially integrated, which was unheard of in the 1930s. Strayhorn, the only black member of the group, experienced the sting of racism on the road and was not even allowed equal accommodations with his colleagues. But, true to form, Strayhorn was not deterred and pursued his musical passion in other avenues that opened up and adhered to his personal mantra: *ever up and onward.*

His skills as a small-group leader would later serve him well during his career with Duke Ellington. In addition to composing and arranging for the Ellington big band, Strayhorn also led sessions under his own name as conductor and performer of small-group projects.

Twentieth-century polls place "Lush Life," composed during this time, as one of the century's top torch songs. Cited by critics, musicians, producers, and music lovers as Strayhorn's seminal work, it remains a wonder to many that he composed it during his teen years.

Duke Ellington remarked that "Lush Life" was a perfect marriage of words and music. "Lush Life" technically rivals the works of great composers from George Gershwin to Stephen Sondheim. Strayhorn

"All music is beautiful," Billy once said to his nieces and nephews. Ellington trombonist Lawrence Brown observed: "All of his tunes have a deep feeling behind them; you hear him in his music, which is the mark of a real musician."

From his high school days Billy was a Francophile. He was fluent in the language and was thrilled with every trip he could make. Aaron Bridgers said, "Nobody cared who you were or what you were. There was no judgment. That's one of the reasons Billy and I loved it here." A photo of the photographer at Versailles was likely made by Bridgers.

"MANY COMPOSERS IN JAZZ ARE VERY GOOD AT THINKING VERTICALLY AND HORIZONTALLY ABOUT MUSIC. BUT BILLY COULD WRITE DIAGONALS AND CURVES AND CIRCLES."

—DONALD SHIRLEY

Billy wrote and arranged great portions of the Broadway show in September and October 1946. His program credit read only "Orchestrations under the personal supervision of Billy Strayhorn." This slight was a turning point in his unwillingness to have his work not acknowledged by Ellington and the press.

Billy takes a break outside Acme Shade and Blind Company in Pittsburgh, around 1937. Around this time, his dreams of becoming a classical pianist dashed, young Strayhorn became "all ears" to recordings of Art Tatum, Teddy Wilson, and Earl Hines.

"VALSE (LENTO SOSTENUTO)" (CA. 1935)

Strayhorn's first love was European concert music, and as a pianist, he naturally gravitated toward the works of Frédéric Chopin. As an accomplished pianist, he must have been intimately familiar with the waltzes, preludes, nocturnes, and mazurkas of the nineteenth-century composer. He was at least familiar enough to try his hand at composing such a waltz himself.

His "Valse (lento sostenuto)" is a masterful exercise in an idiom he did not often work in: classically inspired solo piano music. Though it is somewhat imitative, this juvenile piece is nevertheless brilliantly crafted. Strayhorn cast his attractive theme in a remarkably complex and balanced form. It shows how at a young age, he had already developed a deep understanding of some of music's most abstract elements, such as harmony and structure.

Strayhorn loved waltzes. His amazing adaptation of Ellington's "Mood Indigo" for the 1950 *Masterpieces by Ellington* album carries four fabulous choruses in waltz-time, as does his "Manhattan Murals," an extended version of "Take the 'A' Train." Since waltzes were rather uncommon in jazz, Strayhorn wrote them mostly for his theatrical endeavors, such as *Fantastic Rhythm*, *Beggar's Holiday*, *Jump for Joy*, and *Don Perlimplín*. The Strayhorn waltz Ellington loved best was "Lotus Blossom."

—*Walter van de Leur*

RECOMMENDED RECORDING

⊙ Dutch Jazz Orchestra, *So This Is Love: More Newly Discovered Works of Billy Strayhorn* (Challenge 2002)

BILLY STRAYHORN AND THE FILE CABINETS

Billy Strayhorn became gravely ill and died on May 31, 1967, at the age of fifty-one. His will, drawn up on July 30, 1965, named his nephew, Gregory Morris, as the executor of his estate. Among the few prized possessions that he left behind were a tape recorder and four steel file cabinets.

Alyce Claerbaut (Strayhorn's Niece): When Billy passed away, he lived on Riverside Drive. All of his belongings were being moved, and my brother, Gregory Morris, took possession.

Gregory Morris (Billy Strayhorn's Nephew and Executor): We packed up everything into the trailer and had it taken to the warehouse. Rather than having bureaus and pieces of furniture, Billy kept his shirts, sweaters, and socks in four beautiful steel file cabinets. Being an academic, I asked the family, "May I have the file cabinets that belonged to Uncle Billy?"

On closer inspection at the warehouse, the family found hundreds of elaborately transcribed musical manuscripts impeccably arranged under Strayhorn's clothes.

GM: All of Billy's music manuscripts were in the cabinets, and I took possession of them.

Back in Pittsburgh, Gregory Morris examined the contents of the cabinets. The newly discovered song manuscripts appeared to have been composed by Billy Strayhorn alone. Uncertain about the legal status of the music, the family prepared for an inquiry from the Ellington organization. What happened next in a hotel room astonished Strayhorn's executor.

GM: Duke Ellington really wasn't interested in the material because it represented the past, and Ellington was always looking forward. Billy Strayhorn, his soul mate, was gone, and I didn't think that he was at a point where he could deal with any of the material.

Gregory Morris continued to diligently organize and study the materials.

GM: Nothing was clear about the relationship between Billy Strayhorn to the Ellington organization and Tempo Music until after going through boxes and boxes—literally hundreds and hundreds of pieces of paper. I found a stock agreement—ten shares of stock. Billy Strayhorn owned ten shares of stock in Tempo Music. Billy Strayhorn was a 10 percent owner of Tempo Music.

Another startling surprise was the presence of two hundred newly discovered original Strayhorn compositions: thousands of pages of handwritten manuscripts in such excellent condition that they could readily become complete performance scores.

GM: We then copyrighted over two hundred Strayhorn works.

AC: There were so many songs that were written, even while Billy was working for Ellington. But Billy was careful to keep these new manuscripts in his own private collection.

was so far ahead of his time that some of his compositions were not usable by the Ellington orchestra. "Lush Life" was never recorded or performed by Ellington—never part of the Ellington book. The same can be said of "Valse" which is reminiscent of a Chopin nocturne in its classical Romantic allusions. "Valse" and other newly discovered works uncovered by Van de Leur's research in the 1990s establish the incredible range of Strayhorn's genius as a composer.

Aside from Duke Ellington's prowess as a musician, he was an incredible scout for talent. And when he had the chance to hear Strayhorn display some of his talent, he immediately picked up on these diverse and powerful abilities that Strayhorn possessed and tirelessly honed. Duke knew he had found someone to hold on to.

> *The list of one hundred greatest songs in the last century came out, and "Take the 'A' Train," "Satin Doll," and "Lush Life" were on it. Well, that said an awful lot about Billy Strayhorn's contributions to the world of music.*

All of my life, there's been a controversy about how much credit Billy deserved or who wrote what. And among scholars more recently, it's become a point of debate.

GM: I then extended invitations to many experts to come by and see all of the work I had and to help out with it.

Walter van de Leur (Musicologist and Author): While I was working at the Smithsonian, people said, "You know Billy Strayhorn's family is in Pittsburgh, and Gregory Morris, his nephew, who is the executor of the estate, appears to have found new original materials that came from Strayhorn's apartment. Maybe you want to contact him."

GM: Few people came by except for the young Dutch scholar Walter van de Leur, who was working at the Smithsonian and had done his master's level investigation on Duke Ellington. But when he kept hearing about Billy Strayhorn, he decided that he needed to find out more.

WVDL: I went to Pittsburgh and said, "Wow!" It was paradise, because all the work that I had not been able to locate at the Smithsonian in the Duke Ellington collection and that we had big questions about—"Take the 'A' Train": Is that really Billy Strayhorn? "Chelsea Bridge," "Upper Manhattan Medical Group," "Rain Check"—the important scores were missing from the Ellington collection, and it suggested there was a possibility that they were authored by someone else. And they were all in the Pittsburgh collection.

GM: There were compositions in my possession where the authorship was ambiguous. The actual copyright that followed only had Ellington's name, not Billy Strayhorn's name.

Walter spent an awful lot of time working with those manuscripts, doing research and trying to identify what belonged to Strayhorn and, more importantly, coming up with a way that we could distinguish or identify the Strayhorn musical footprint.

The list of one hundred greatest songs in the last century came out, and "Take the 'A' Train," "Satin Doll," and "Lush Life" were on it. Well, that said an awful lot about Billy Strayhorn's contributions to the world of music.

—Robert Levi

THE STANLEY THEATER

It was a chilly day on December 1, 1938, a day that would change Billy's life forever. Duke Ellington was coming to Pittsburgh to perform at the Stanley Theater. A classmate of Billy's introduced him to another student, George Greenlee, whose uncle was Augustus "Gus" Greenlee. Gus was a very influential black man whose success in several rackets made him a player in the black power elite society. Gus knew Duke Ellington, and through the prodding of his nephew George, Gus set up a meeting to introduce Billy to Ellington. Billy had been granted a brief interview after the show in Duke's dressing room. Upon arriving in Ellington's dressing room, George introduced the two. Ellington was having his hair conked, or as we might say today, processed. Duke with his

Billy stopped for some Schweppervescence while traveling. Good enough for the British royal family, good enough for Billy.

A LOOK AT STRAYHORN'S LIFE IN PITTSBURGH

Billy Strayhorn was born on November 29, 1915, in Dayton, Ohio. His family later moved to Pittsburgh's predominantly black Homewood section. During a rough stretch in his infancy, Billy became gravely ill. His sister Lillian recalls:

Lillian Strayhorn (Billy Strayhorn's Sister): Bill had the whooping cough and rickets, and they became debilitating. And with the rickets, his legs were bowed. Doctors recommended that my mother have his legs broken and reset. And someone told her, "No, honey, you don't have to do that." She said, "Every evening, after you get through washing your dishes, stand him up in the dishpan and rub his legs down with that greasy soapy water." That's what my mother did. And then he got the straightest legs of all of us: nice straight legs. So I asked my mother, "Why didn't you stand *me* up in the dishpan?"

Later on as a teenager, Billy began to develop his own distinct style.

LS: Classmates sometimes called Billy "Dictionary." Whenever they needed an explanation for anything they would always ask him. They didn't have to go to find the dictionary.

Billy was also an excellent English student. Teachers took a particular liking to him and suggested what he ought to read. In those days, your English classes were founded on the classics, so you had to have read *Silas Marner* and Shakespeare.

Fred Hersch (Pianist, Bandleader, and Composer): Billy Strayhorn grew up in a dirt floor house in Pittsburgh—how he got to where he got is just one of those great, amazing American stories. By all rights, Strayhorn should have remained unknown, but he had imagination, he had drive, and he had ambition.

Young Billy delivered newspapers and toiled long hours in a drugstore so he could earn enough money to buy sheet music and even a piano.

LS: Billy was a soda jerk and a delivery person at the Pennfield Pharmacy. He'd wear a white jacket. And he'd get me an ice cream cone and tell me to go back home. They didn't need to see some little dusty child running around up there in this pharmacy, because there weren't any black kids up there. But at that time, I wasn't thinking about that; I was just going up there to see my brother and get an ice cream cone!

As Billy's music became more sophisticated, so did his sense of style and appearance.

LS: The cologne! He had a wonderful signature scent that smelled so rich. I wore it for years myself! It was Tailspin. He had such style with the clothes he wore. He was fastidious and never cut the pockets of his suits because he wouldn't carry much in his pockets. Why? That could ruin the line and the look.

One time Billy came home with a beautiful suit, and my brothers were saying, "Ooh, that's very unusual." It was an unusual color, and Billy said, "Oh, that's because it's the wrong side of the fabric." Billy said, "I had a fellow make it for me, and he accidentally turned it over and made it on the wrong side." We said, "Why didn't you straighten him out?" Billy said, "No, no, no! I like it this way—it's gorgeous!" And it was!

Herb Jordan (Writer and Composer): Billy was a master musician when he left Pittsburgh. By the time he met Duke Ellington, he was already fully formed as a composer. If you look at the songs he brought from Pittsburgh, including "Day Dream" and "Something to Live For," you'll see that some of his best work was created prior to meeting Duke Ellington.

—Robert Levi

Strayhorn should have remained unknown, but he had imagination, he had drive, and he had ambition.

TAKE THE 'A' TRAIN
by BILLY STRAYHORN

TEMPO MUSIC, INC.
Sole Selling Agents
PACIFIC MUSIC SALES
TEMPO MUSIC, INC.
HOLLYWOOD, BROADWAY
NEW YORK CITY

Strayhorn acknowledged the influence of Fletcher Henderson on "'A' Train." He initially tossed the song out, worrying that it was too derivative; Mercer Ellington rescued the score.

eyes closed never looked at Billy. He only ordered him to sit down at the piano and said, "Let me hear what you can do."

Billy, not a bit reserved, sat down and turned toward Duke and said, "Mr. Ellington, this is the way you performed 'Sophisticated Lady' in the show." He proceeded to play the song note for note exactly as Ellington had just played it in the show. After completing the number, he then said to the Duke, "Now this is the way I would play it," at which time he started changing keys, revising the tempo, and shifting into a very "cool" sound.

As Strayhorn turned at the end of the tune, Ellington was standing directly behind him. For the first time

LILLIAN STRAYHORN DICKS

SISTER

I don't know how to explain my brother Bill. He was like something out of a fantastical story. You know the fairy tales, where they take the newborn baby away, and they put another one in its place, and they call it a changeling? Well, that's what Bill was like. He wasn't like any other person in our family. He wasn't like any other person in the world. It was like he came from somewhere else.

He was so centered, so focused. He always looked you in the eye, and it was like he was looking right through you.

In the house, it was like he occupied a different space than everyone else. He was there but wasn't there. That's the best way I know to describe him: he was there but wasn't there.

I'm not saying that he was perfect, mind you. He had his little quirks. I'd like to give you an example.

The thing I remember most about him was his always being at the piano. He was also so meticulous, very particular about how he looked. He would never allow his pants to be wrinkled. Consequently, he hardly ever sat down at the piano in his pants. He always took his pants off and hung them, so he wouldn't wrinkle them. He sat at the piano in his undershorts and shoes and socks, and he played.

My mother would say, "Bill, for God's sake, put on some clothes."

But he didn't want to wrinkle his pants. He'd say, "I am wearing clothes, Mama. Underpants and socks are clothes."

As told to David Hajdu

Photograph circa 1943. Ellington recalled that Billy's laughter impressed him as much as his playing did on their first meeting.

"LUSH LIFE" (CA. 1936)

That a youngster from one of Pittsburgh's poorest and most depressing neighborhoods came up with "Lush Life," one of jazz's most beloved ballads, is baffling. Strayhorn started to work on the song sometime in his late teens and must have completed it by 1936. He paired sophisticated lyrics with an exquisite yet pretty complex musical setting, which put him in the same league as some of his much older contemporaries: Gershwin, Porter, Berlin.

The clever, inner-rhyming first stanza is absolutely brilliant: *"I used to visit all the very gay places / Those come-what-may places / Where one relaxes on the axis of the wheel of life / To get the feel of life / from jazz and cocktails."*

Next, he bespeaks his love of the French language in what are possibly the most often mangled lines in jazz:

"The girls I knew had sad and sullen grey faces / with distingué traces / That used to be there you could see where they'd been washed away / By too many through the day / Twelve o'clock tales."

These memories that hint at the Roaring Twenties give way to the grim present, where "life is lonely again." "A week in Paris might ease the bite of it," the protagonist muses but to no avail, and in the end, he is with "those whose lives are lonely too."

In 1949, singer-pianist Nat King Cole premiered Strayhorn's "Lush Life" on record, the first of countless performances and recordings by jazz vocalists and instrumentalists. Others, too, have tried their hands at it, from Queen Latifah to Lady Gaga. Among the most rewarding renditions are those rare ones recorded by the pianist-composer himself, such as the 1964 version from *Basin Street East*. Though his singing is slightly out of tune, Strayhorn delivers the song with just enough subtle irony to steer it away from becoming a too-heavy torch song.

—Walter van de Leur

RECOMMENDED RECORDINGS

- Billy Strayhorn, *Lush Life* (1964; Red Barron 1992)
- John Coltrane, *Lush Life* (Prestige 1960)

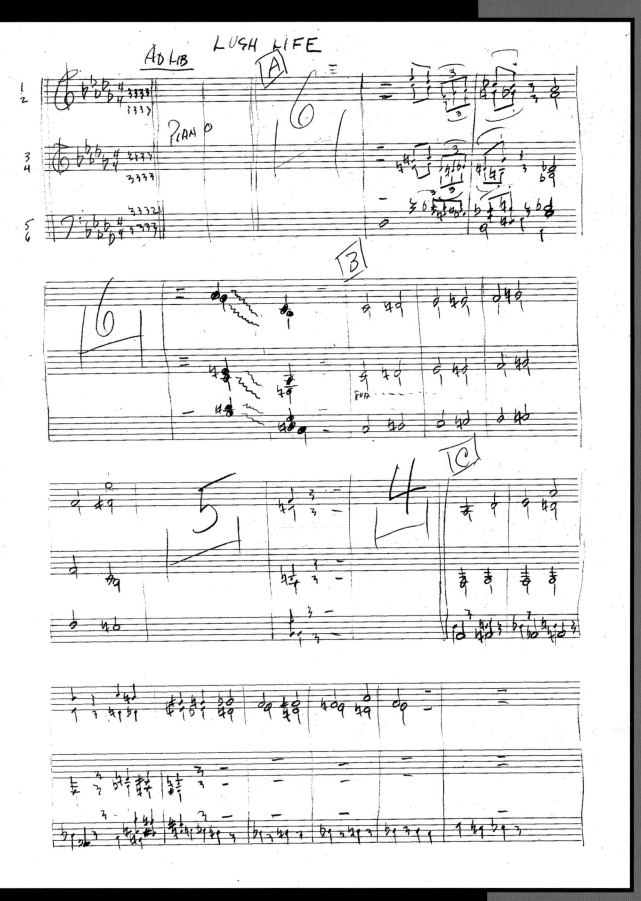

"'Lush Life' is a widely recorded ballad, but in 1963, the unlikely duo of John Coltrane and Johnny Hartman collaborated to produce one of its most celebrated renditions. The story goes that the two Johns heard Nat King Cole singing 'Lush Life' on the radio as they prepared to record an album together, and both men immediately decided to include the tune. The song would become a standard in my Uncle Johnny's performances, and his most cherished accolade was what Strayhorn told him about the recording: 'Johnny, you did this song exactly how I meant it.'" *Hermene Hartman, niece of Johnny Hartman.*

The honorable Gerald Lascelles, Al Celley, Billy Strayhorn, Duke Ellington, and the Earl of Harewood on the QEII on the way to the Leeds Festival, 1958.

"SOMETHING TO LIVE FOR" (CA. 1937)

One of the final known works to come out of Strayhorn's Pittsburgh years was his torch song "Something to Live For." The first verse starts out with some light ironic touches: *"I have almost everything a human could desire / Cars and houses, bearskin rugs to lie before my fire."*

And then the song becomes more plangent in the ensuing lines: *"But there's something missing, something isn't there / It seems I'm never kissing / The one whom I could care for."*

These lyrics hint at a somber personal truth that stretched further than romantic love. The youngster who wrote these lines actually had many more unfulfilled desires. He may have been extremely gifted musically, but it was not possible for a black man to pursue a career in European classical music. The Broadway-style musical theater that he loved so much was virtually inaccessible to African American composers too. Furthermore, his homosexuality was completely taboo in 1930s America (and in many decades beyond). Strayhorn's years in Pittsburgh were difficult. "'Something to Live For,'" wrote his biographer, David Hajdu, "embodies the whole of his youthful frustration."

—Walter van de Leur

RECOMMENDED RECORDING

○ Lena Horne, *We'll Be Together Again* (Blue Note 1994)

Ellington and Strayhorn made eye contact. Ellington said, "Can you do that again?" When Billy began again several band members had gathered around. Strayhorn played and sang many of his original tunes to the delight of all the listeners. Surely Mr. Ellington was impressed with Billy's musical and technical skills, but what's more is that he sensed that this young man had a marvelous instinct for the music when he played. This was far from common.

In less than two months, on January 23, 1939, Billy was incorporated into the Duke Ellington band. Strayhorn's first job, not surprisingly, was that of lyricist. Ellington hired lyricists to pen words to some of the great tunes for which he is known. Mitchell Parish, who penned the words to "Sophisticated Lady" and other tunes, was one such person. In addition to being a great composer of music, Billy was a wordsmith as is indicated by the songs he wrote before he left Pittsburgh. He was a consummate songwriter. No doubt this was a factor in the success of his play *Fantastic Rhythm*.

In March 1939, the band recorded its first Strayhorn composition, "Something to Live For," from *Fantastic Rhythm*. Duke notably added his name as a co-composer to the song, a practice that unfortunately was repeated many times in the Ellington-Strayhorn collaboration. By the end of 1940, the Ellington band had recorded a total of three Strayhorn tunes, adding "Your Love Has Faded" and "Day Dream." This issue of authorship would raise its head again in the future. Something providential happened, however, early on that enabled Billy to be credited for a string of new compositions he was about to create.

The RCA album *Esquire All-American 1946 Award Winners* featured guest artist Louis Armstrong (vocal and trumpet) and pianists Billy Strayhorn and Duke Ellington. Louis, Billy, and Duke were photographed at the January

Hajdu recounts in his biography that it wasn't uncommon for a friend to stop by and find Strayhorn examining the orchestral score of a classical piece such as Stravinsky's *Rite of Spring* simply for the joy of studying it.

"STRAYHORN LIVES THE LIFE THAT I WOULD LOVE TO LIVE. **YOU KNOW, HE IS THE PURE ARTIST.** HE DOESN'T HAVE TO UH, WELL, HE WRITES WHEN THE SPIRIT STRIKES HIM, AND WHAT HE WRITES IS PURE STRAYHORN, UNADULTERATED, WITHOUT ANY OUTSIDE EFFECTS, I MEAN WITHOUT ANYBODY SCREAMING AT HIM."

—DUKE ELLINGTON IN AN INTERVIEW WITH BOB SMITH ON CBC, NOVEMBER 1, 1962.

"A FLOWER IS A LOVESOME THING" (1939)

Within months of joining Duke Ellington in New York, in the winter of 1939, Strayhorn had written two ballads for Johnny Hodges, the orchestra's star alto saxophonist: "Passion Flower" and "A Flower Is a Lovesome Thing." While there's evidence that "A Flower Is a Lovesome Thing" made it into the band book as early as February 1941, it wasn't until 1946 that the Johnny Hodges All-Stars waxed the piece for Capitol Transcriptions.

There is a kinship between "Passion Flower" and "A Flower Is a Lovesome Thing" that exceeds their botanic titles. Both pieces are built on similar musical ideas, such as very little harmonic movement, a technique found in other pieces as well. Throughout "A Flower Is a Lovesome Thing," Strayhorn maintains a subdued and minor mood. As always, his writing is detailed and effectively expressive of the emotional content of this introspective composition.

—Walter van de Leur

RECOMMENDED RECORDING

⊙ Don Braden, Mark Rapp, *The Strayhorn Project* (Premium Music 2010)

"TAKE THE 'A' TRAIN"

In January 1941 a bitter dispute between members of the American Society of Composers, Authors and Publishers (ASCAP) and the broadcasters caused a ban over the airwaves of ASCAP member music. For the first time, Duke Ellington was not able to play any of his own compositions. Billy, not having joined ASCAP, was suddenly launched into a writing frenzy that would become almost unparalleled in his career. The first Strayhorn song featured in broadcast after the strike began was "Take the 'A' Train." Billy subsequently started pumping out tunes like an assembly line. "Chelsea Bridge," "Clementine," "A Flower Is a Lovesome Thing," "Rain Check," "After All," and "Love Like This Can't Last" were some of the Strayhorn pieces written during the strike. In addition, some fifteen compositions written or adapted for the Blanton-Webster band remained unrecorded until recently.

"Take the 'A' Train" was adopted as the band's theme song in early 1941. In the next few years after the ASCAP strike, Billy was soaring like an eagle. He received the Esquire Silver Award two years in succession—December 1945 and 1946. In addition, he won the *DownBeat* readers poll for arranger of the year in 1946. Another milestone was the recording of his ballad "Lush Life" by the incomparable Nat King Cole. It was the beginning of a string of artists who would record the great ballad.

LENA HORNE

In 1941, Billy spent a year in California. Aside from meeting many well-known stars, one very special relationship developed that would last the rest of his life.

September 13, 1950, Ellington bassist Oscar Pettiford led a recording of Billy's most popular composition using cello instead of his traditional instrument. It was perhaps the second recorded use of cello in jazz and led to broader exploration of its possibilities as a jazz solo instrument. Billy's celeste playing adds to the arresting reinterpretation.

He was given the enormous task of being a chaperone for the lovely Ms. Lena Horne. They became soul mates almost instantly and were just about inseparable. Ms. Horne describes it this way in David Hajdu's biography: "For me it was as if my other self came up and spoke to me—we were that much in sync." Strayhorn worked closely with Lena to refine her singing style. He had a special way with singers and tended to be a boost to their confidence. After three or four

"TAKE THE 'A' TRAIN" (1939)

As conductor and historian Gunther Schuller admitted in the 2007 *Independent Lens* documentary that celebrated the life and music of Billy Strayhorn: "I have heard 'Take the "A" Train'—what—ten thousand times? To this day it is hard for me to fully accept that it was a Strayhorn composition. But, my God, this piece is so pure Ellington. That is really staggering." Schuller is far from alone in finding it difficult to accept that Strayhorn wrote the Ellington orchestra's post-1940 signature theme.

Yet Ellington, who otherwise loved to lay smoke screens, was remarkably clear when it came to the origins of "'A' Train." At numerous concerts and in many interviews, he invariably pointed out that not he, but his collaborator Billy Strayhorn was the composer of his band's famous theme.

When the Smithsonian Institution acquired Ellington's papers in 1988, scholars finally had a chance to study his composition methods and to answer questions of authorship. However, for "'A' Train" they drew a blank: no original score surfaced, which led to all kinds of speculation and rumors. Yet the work's absence in itself hinted at its author. Even though many Strayhorn contributions had ended up in the Ellington orchestra's library, Strayhorn seemed to have kept the music that was most dear to him in his own apartment. "Take the 'A' Train" was among these items, and it is still in the possession of his estate. The full score in Billy Strayhorn's hand is reproduced here for the first time.

These three pages, sketchy as they may seem, contain everything needed for the Ellington band to perform the work in all its glory.* The orchestra's countless renditions of "'A'" Train in the decades following its composition are all by and large based on this modest-looking three-staff autograph: one for the saxes, one for the trumpets, and one for the trombones and double-bass. True, the performance is at slight variance with Strayhorn's score. Some voices were doubled and some notes were shortened, as was customary. While extracting the individual band parts, Strayhorn made some slight final adaptations. Furthermore, there are some things missing: the famous piano introduction, the rhythm section parts (piano, bass, drums), a rescored eight-bar brass background, the trumpet solo, and the two-bar ending. But none of these omissions or differences are worth much concern.

Piano introductions were never written out, and likewise no document has survived for the opening bars of "'A' Train." Strayhorn in all likelihood is the author, because his piano introductions typically used musical ideas set forth in the piece, as is the case here. The intro centers on the theme's famous whole-tone chord in bar two and the metric shifts that shape some of the material (for instance at the break at the end of the trumpet solo).

Rhythm section parts were typically worked out on the bandstand and are hardly ever in the score. Omitting these parts from this particular score is completely consistent with the orchestra's standard methods.

The rescored eight-bar brass background of the first chorus can be found on Strayhorn's surviving handwritten instrumental parts in the hand of copyist Juan Tizol. The author is unknown, but it must be Strayhorn. Both the voice leading of these new brass chords and the rhythmic patterns are in keeping with his earlier and later work.

Ray Nance's masterly solo on "'A' Train" isn't notated either, as was customary for ad-lib solos. His solo is built on embellishments and variations of the tune, which Strayhorn had penciled in his part for reference.

Finally, the two closing bars that are missing from the autograph use a simple swing era cliché that was readily available for anyone looking for a quick tag.

In spite of all the overwhelming evidence that "'A' Train" is by Strayhorn, those who have difficulty accepting that have come up with elaborate theories why the piece still is Ellington's. He must have dictated it to Strays (preferably from the bath tub); the score is really a copy of Duke's now-lost original; its success owes largely to Ellingtonian improvements of what was nothing more than an unfinished sketch; and other far-fetched schemes that are completely at odds with the working routines of both composers.

Strayhorn composed "'A' Train" not long after he had first met Ellington in December 1938. That earlier autograph, which Mercer Ellington claims to have rescued from the trash, is apparently lost. The famous score reproduced here is from January 1941. Interestingly, the saxophone section of the second chorus does hint at its earlier origins. Strayhorn quite atypically left out Ben Webster, who joined in 1940.[†]

"The reason we gave it that title," Strayhorn explained, "was because they were building the Sixth Avenue subway at that time, and they added new trains, including the 'D' Train, which came up to Harlem, to 145th Street, and then turned off and went to the Bronx, but the 'A' Train kept straight on up to 200-and-something Street. People got confused. They'd take the 'D' Train, and it would go to Harlem and 145th Street, but the next stop would be in the Bronx. So I said I was writing directions—take the 'A' Train to Sugar Hill."

"Take the 'A' Train" stands out in Strayhorn's (and Ellington's!) repertoire as a rather unusual work, because it is more in keeping with swing era conventions than with Strayhorn's own compositional style and musical vocabulary. Calling up the sounds of a New York subway train rushing through the tunnels, "'A' Train" is mostly about movement. The ride begins with the famous be-bop-flavored saxophone theme against snappy brass answers, followed by whirling section work in the next choruses, from rolling saxophone chords under Ray Nance's trumpet solo to offbeat plunger-muted brass interjections in the final chorus. For contrast, Strayhorn shifts gears with a vigorous four-bar transition at the end of the trumpet solo section. Later the forward motion comes to a temporary halt with a rhythmically displaced cross-section bell-chord that aptly evokes the train's horn bouncing off the underground walls.

The February 1941 recording of the tune became one of the band's biggest commercial successes, and consequently Ellington adopted "'A' Train" in the fall of that year as the band's signature theme.

—Walter van de Leur

RECOMMENDED RECORDINGS

● Duke Ellington and His Famous Orchestra, *The Blanton-Webster Band* (RCA Bluebird 56)

● Michel Petrucciani, *Non-Stop Travels With Michel Petrucciani/Trio Live In Stuttgart* (Dreyfus)

* For a detailed description of score writing in the Ellington orchestra see Van de Leur, *Something to Live For: The Music of Billy Strayhorn*, Oxford UP 2002, and "'People Wrap Their Lunches in Them': Duke Ellington and His Written Music Manuscripts," in John Howland (ed.), *Duke Ellington Studies Anthology*, Cambridge UP, 2015.

† This section is quite flawed in Schuller's edition of the score—there are other oversights in his version as well.

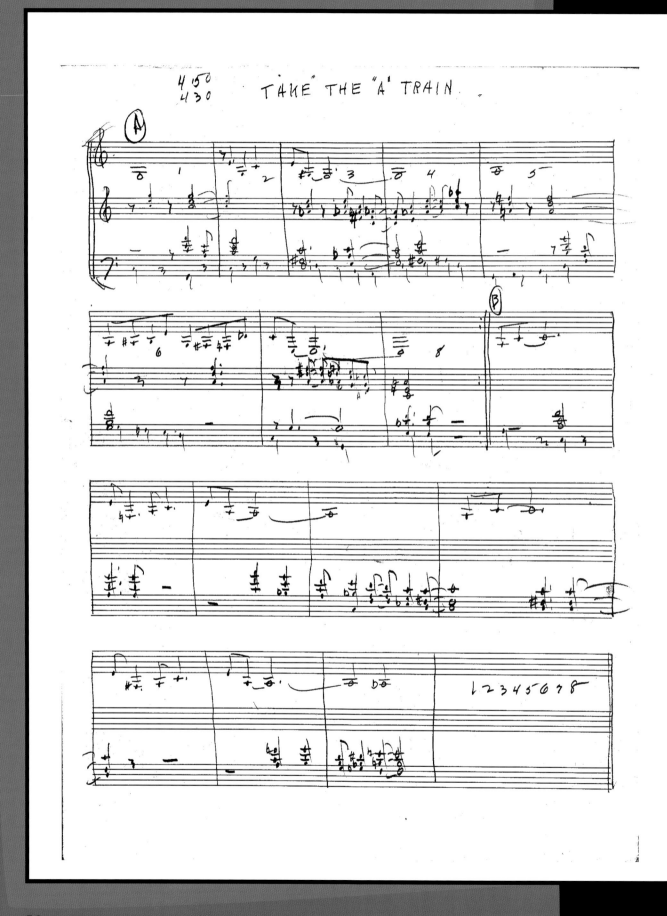

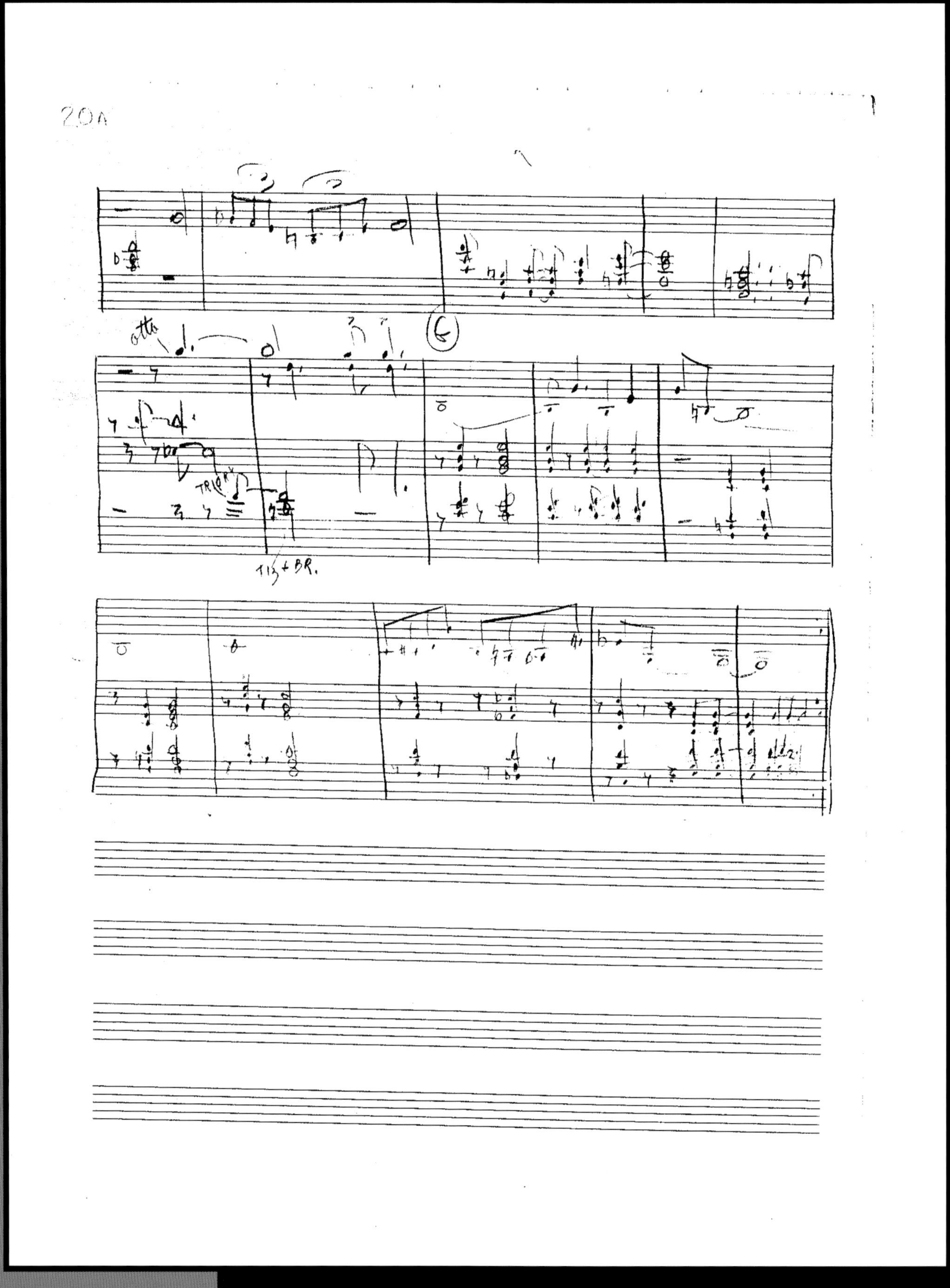
20A

A composite poster created by Pittsburgh photographer Fred Kenderson using a manuscript score of "Take the 'A' Train."

"Billy Strayhorn was always the most unselfish, the most patient, and the most imperturbable, no matter how dark the day. I am indebted to him for so much of my courage since 1939. He was my listener, my most dependable appraiser, and as a critic he would be the most clinical, but his background—both classical and modern—was an accessory to his own good taste and understanding." *Duke Ellington*

Grandmother Lizzie was a major musical influence on Billy. She also infected him with her love of flowers. "A Flower Is a Lovesome Thing" was far more than a song title. Flowers fascinated Strayhorn, inspiring a significant number of his songs. He loved gifting them to his favorite women, Lena and Marian Bruce Logan.

weeks of constant companionship, Lena and Billy were even closer. They went on walks, to restaurants and clubs—they had experienced something special. Again Ms. Horne is quoted: "I wanted to marry him so badly. He was just everything that I wanted in a man, except he wasn't interested in me sexually. We were in love anyway. He was the only man I really loved." Billy had assumed a gay lifestyle shortly after arriving in New York City.

The 1940s were a good time for Billy because big bands were thriving in that decade. The challenge would come in the '50s for big bands in general and for Billy specifically. The string of songs that Strayhorn produced during the ASCAP strike would prove to be critical to the legacy of Billy Strayhorn because even though he wrote them in the '40s, which was primarily the big band era, those compositions lent themselves to the cutting-edge style of jazz that was soon to be created in the '50s, known as bebop. Today young artists are recording new versions of those songs because of their adaptation to bebop. Billy was ahead of his time. He hung out with the architects of bebop such as Dizzy Gillespie and Thelonious Monk. He "traded the dozens" on piano with Monk at a club in

Harlem called Minton's. His artistry spread throughout the jazz community. As Ellington had a wide legacy and was highly revered in the general public, Strayhorn's legacy was equally revered within the music industry itself.

In 1947, Lena Horne decided to marry a longtime boyfriend, Lennie Hayton. Lennie was an arranger and conductor for MGM and a onetime pianist for the Paul Whiteman Orchestra. Lena had submitted Lennie to Billy for his approval, and he gave it. Billy accompanied them to Paris, France, where they were married on April 16. Billy made frequent visits to their apartment, often staying up until the wee hours of the morning—talking and playing music. Lennie was contemplating starting his own publishing company, and he questioned Strayhorn about his agreement with Ellington. He was quite surprised to find out that Billy had none. Indeed he had no clue as to what his arrangements and compositions might bring in if shopped in the marketplace. Lennie encouraged Billy to pursue

Billy soaks up the Palm Springs sun during a visit to Lena Horne's California home. Photo from the early 1960s.

a more definitive business relationship with Ellington. Strayhorn and Ellington did talk, but Billy had looked into his royalties and was unhappy. Strayhorn pulled away, causing some distance in the relationship.

"PASSION FLOWER" (1939)

Billy Strayhorn wrote "Passion Flower" in 1939, shortly after starting his new gig with Duke's band. As such, it was the first in a string of emotionally involved ballads he wrote for altoist Johnny Hodges. Hodges first recorded "Passion Flower" in 1941 with a small band drawn from the orchestra, after which it gradually became something of a signature tune for the altoist.

Harmonically and melodically, the work is consistent with Strayhorn's earlier Pittsburgh works but quite removed from Ellington's writing. Like many other works from the period, "Passion Flower" points out Strayhorn's admiration for and study of the French "impressionist" composer Claude Debussy. "Passion Flower" is one of those pieces that will thrill listeners with a

knack for complex sounds since Strayhorn managed to pack some highly advanced harmonic techniques in the song. This adds an extra musical layer—the tension one feels throughout—which is characteristic of many of Strayhorn's works. There is beauty but inner conflict as well, which allows one to hear different aspects each time the song plays.

—Walter van de Leur

RECOMMENDED RECORDING

⊙ Fred Hersch, *Passion Flower: Fred Hersch Plays Billy Strayhorn* (Nonesuch 1996)

PASSION FLOWER

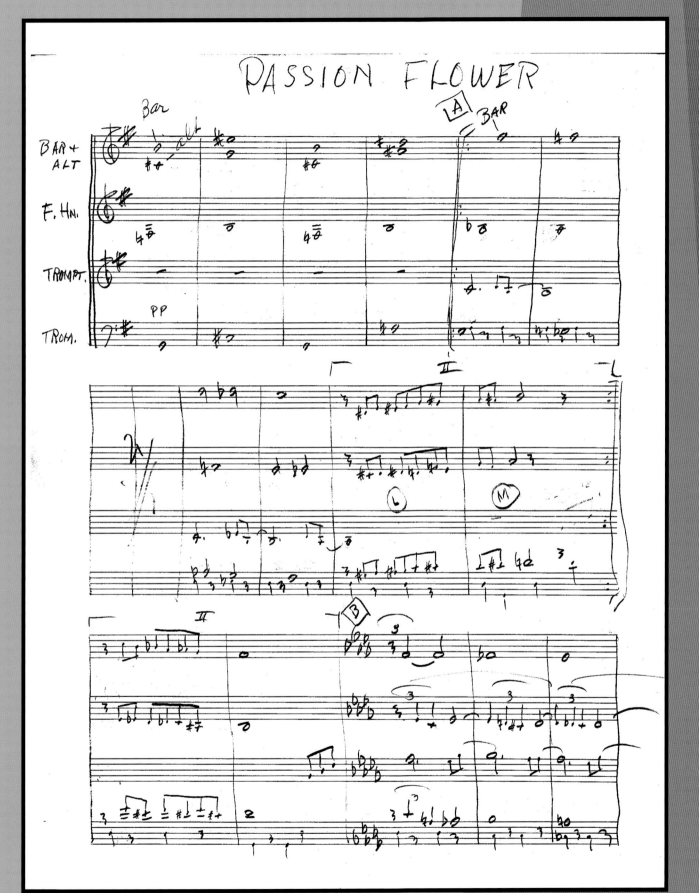

The Haytons—Lennie and Lena Horne—pictured with Billy for the 1962 Copasetics' *Anchors Aweigh*. Of the benefit shows Rachel (Mrs. Jackie) Robinson said, "Anybody who was anybody had to be there." Miles Davis attended, as did Willie Mays, and always Arthur and Marian Bruce Logan. "People waited all year for the next Copasetics night," Robinson continued. "It was important to the community—all that talent dedicated to doing something good for the community, and no profit motive. You felt wonderful being a part of it." Ellington was conspicuous in his absence.

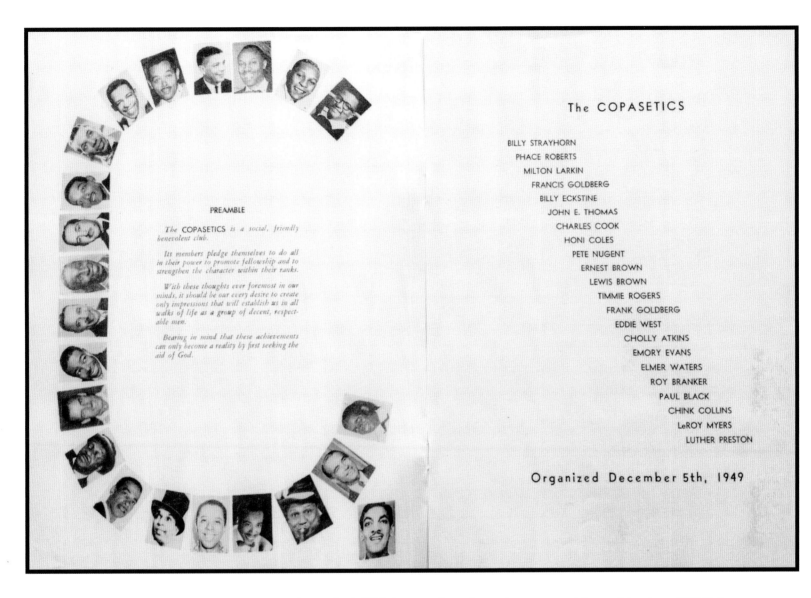

PREAMBLE

The COPASETICS is a social, friendly benevolent club.

Its members pledge themselves to do all in their power to promote fellowship and to strengthen the character within their ranks.

With these thoughts ever foremost in our minds, it should be our every desire to create only impressions that will establish us in all walks of life as a group of decent, respectable men.

Bearing in mind that these achievements can only become a reality by first seeking the aid of God.

The COPASETICS

BILLY STRAYHORN

PHACE ROBERTS

MILTON LARKIN

FRANCIS GOLDBERG

BILLY ECKSTINE

JOHN E. THOMAS

CHARLES COOK

HONI COLES

PETE NUGENT

ERNEST BROWN

LEWIS BROWN

TIMMIE ROGERS

FRANK GOLDBERG

EDDIE WEST

CHOLLY ATKINS

EMORY EVANS

ELMER WATERS

ROY BRANKER

PAUL BLACK

CHINK COLLINS

LeROY MYERS

LUTHER PRESTON

Organized December 5th, 1949

Strayhorn was a founding member of the Copasetics in 1950. A group of mostly tap dancers, associates, and devotees of Bill "Bojangles" Robinson, they gathered as a fraternity and staged events to benefit charities. Their annual September dance, featuring music composed by Strayhorn, was a highlight of the Harlem calendar.

THE COPASETICS

The early '50s was a new era for Billy. He began to work independently from the Duke. The Copasetics was a social club in New York that met once a week in rotating locations. It was a black gathering of dancers and entertainers created in honor of the late dancer Bill "Bojangles" Robinson. Billy accepted an invitation to join in 1950 and was received with open arms. They all accepted him as a peer and soon elected him president of the group. His first order of business was to write music for the members to perform. He did this by composing annual revues for the group. It was a social club, but it was also an

RUTH ELLINGTON BOATWRIGHT

SISTER OF DUKE ELLINGTON

I always called him Billums. I always called my brother Edward. When Billums moved to New York, he didn't have anywhere to stay. He was living at the Y. So we invited him to move into our family home in Harlem, where Duke and I lived with my nephew Mercer.

In our home, Billums was always at the piano, and when he wasn't at the piano, he was thinking about music. Sometimes he would be writing music at night and would fall asleep over the manuscript, sitting at the table. And then he would wake up and start writing again.

He was very protective of me and had to approve all my boyfriends, in terms of their character. He insisted on meeting every one of them. He would sit them down in the living room and talk. He smiled charmingly and chatted about nothing in particular. He appeared to be having a charming social conversation, and all the time he was analyzing them to see what they were made of. He was very clever, extremely brilliant, and extremely profound.

> In our home, Billums was always at the piano, and when he wasn't at the piano, he was thinking about music.

The one thing that stands out with me about Billy is that no matter what anyone did, he never was concerned with anyone trying to hurt him, and he was always understanding and sympathetic and seeing every point of view, without any reference to himself whatsoever. He had the most objective mind of anyone I've ever seen and no self-consciousness at all, and no fear of what anyone could do to him. I don't know anybody else who has that. If I saw that somebody hadn't done right by him, he'd say, "Oh, darling, don't worry about it," and he'd just go on. That was a great thing about Billums. He was always very sane.

As told to David Hajdu

organization that actively provided opportunities to raise money for causes, mainly the Harlem Hospital. Duke Ellington's physician, Arthur Logan, was an influential physician at Harlem Hospital. He and his wife, Marian, were very supportive of all kinds of social and political causes in Harlem. Billy was the only member who was not a dancer. He created revues for no fewer than thirteen annual Copasetics benefit shows. These little song and dance shows provided performance opportunities for the hoofers who were often out of work due to discriminatory practices in the dance world. Honi Coles and Talley Beatty were members of the Copasetics. The Copasetics (which still exists today) was also involved in the civil rights movement of the 1960s. Billy wrote a revue in 1963 in advance of the March on Washington called "Down Dere." Scores for that work unfortunately did not survive.

Earl "Fatha" Hines, Billy Strayhorn, and Bob Dews, backstage at the Pittsburgh Civic Arena, June 1965. *Photograph by Charles "Teenie" Harris, American, 1908–1998, Kodak Safety Film, H: 4 in. x W: 5 in., Carnegie Museum of Art, Pittsburgh, Heinz Family Fund.*

"From a 1947 recording session for Al Hall's short-lived Wax label, where Billy played bongos. The pianist was Jimmy Jones, and the bassist is Billy Taylor Jr., whose more famous father had been with Duke. On the same day (though exact recording dates for Wax are unknown) Billy Sr. and Jimmy also recorded with Ellingtonians Hodges, Brown, and Carney, with Billy quite probably the arranger—there was no band or leader name on the labels." –Dan Morgenstern

Billy also collaborated with Duke Ellington on a number of theatrical works, including *Jump for Joy* (1941), a satire on race relations in the United States, and *Beggar's Holiday* (1946), based on the 1782 John Gay work *Beggar's Opera*. Strayhorn was not credited for the massive number of songs he wrote for these pieces. Many of them still survive, but both productions had difficulty getting off the ground. Although *Jump for Joy* ran for several weeks in Los Angeles, it never went to Broadway after that.

"DAY DREAM" (1939)

While Ellington was away on his second European tour, Strayhorn was in his new hometown of New York City. "I stayed at home and wrote a few things, like 'Day Dream,'" he later explained. Given the date of composition, the bridge ("don't know the time," etc.) is harmonically quite advanced, as it is based on a chord technique that later became central in post-war bebop compositions. Years later, Sonny Rollins used the same chords in the bridge of his 1954 "Airegin"; even the melody is virtually the same.

Undoubtedly, one of Strayhorn's finest arrangements for the 1956 *Ella Fitzgerald Sings the Duke Ellington Songbook* sessions is his breathtaking score of "Day Dream." Strayhorn smartly parallels the airy and sensual atmosphere of John LaTouche's lyrics with a beautifully rich orchestration. For instance, as if to mirror the experience of dreaming while being awake, Strayhorn refers to so-called polychords—chords that relate to two different tonal centers simultaneously—as if they are awake but dreaming. The score opens with a succession of wrenching polychords, which results in an ethereal passage with sharply dissonant, hazy clouds of sound.

The remainder of the score is equally successful. Against Ella's crystalline voice, Strayhorn scored a warm background suggestive of the ebb and flow of breathing in and out. Orchestral voices move from dissonant to consonant chord tones, continuously altering the color and weight of the harmonies. It provides a steady pulse of tension and relaxation.

–Walter van de Leur

RECOMMENDED RECORDING

⦿ Ella Fitzgerald, *Ella Fitzgerald Sings the Duke Ellington Songbook* (Verve 1956)

DAY DREAM

THE FILE CABINETS AND NEWLY DISCOVERED SONGS

Alyce Claerbaut: "Valse," which is Billy's Chopin-like piano piece, was written in 1934. And when he died in 1967, that piece, in its original form, was among his personal effects. That he would keep it that long was remarkable—it was a part of his own storehouse of life.

Bill Charlap (Pianist and Bandleader): In "Valse," you can hear his knowledge of classical music and of Chopin. But there's also a little bit of ragtime in there; "Valse" has got a little bit of both classical and ragtime in it to my ear.

Terell Stafford (Trumpeter, Bandleader, and Composer): When I hear Billy Strayhorn's music and then hear Chopin's music, to me they're similar in a way: each composer has an affinity for melody and how melody can evoke emotion.

Herb Jordan: The notion that a young black man from Pittsburgh could be either a classical composer or a classical pianist was absurd in 1935. There were no opportunities, and there was no place for Strayhorn to go as either a composer or a pianist.

BC: Another newly found composition, "Sprite Music," is one of Strayhorn's impressionist works, and you can hear Debussy and Ravel in it. Strayhorn had quite a musical mind!

Luther Henderson (Composer, Arranger, and Orchestrator): There was also a song in the famous Broadway show *Beggar's Holiday* called "Brown Penny" that was discovered by Strayhorn's biographer in one of his file cabinets. It was written well before he joined up with Duke Ellington.

—Robert Levi

Other theatrical works by Ellington and Strayhorn were *Saturday Laughter* (1958), based on *Mine Boy*, a novel by Peter Abrahams on South African apartheid, and Orson Welles's ill-fated work *Faust* (1953). However, there are songs that Billy wrote that still survive. Nevertheless, he became very embittered when he was removed from any acknowledgment of any writing beyond the orchestrations. It was this particular incident that helped fuel his walking away from Ellington in the '50s.

In addition to doing projects with the Copasetics, Billy worked on a version of *Cabin in the Sky* and the Federico García Lorca classic *The Love of Don Perlimplín and Belisa in the Garden*. Four songs from the latter are now performed by the Dutch Jazz Orchestra—"Sprite Music," "The Flowers Die of Love," "Love, Love," and "Wounded Love." Billy Strayhorn teamed up with his Juilliard-trained friend Luther Henderson in the summer of 1954 to collaborate on a musical. He had his sights set on Broadway. One of the discussions centered on looking at the world through rose-colored glasses. They decided that their theme would focus on: What's reality? What's perception? What's the difference? Together they called their brainchild *Rose-Colored Glasses*. For the show they pooled songs from their respective archives and wrote some new numbers. Both musicians felt they could bring in some significant money through the performances.

Strayhorn broke the news of their project to Ellington. Billy was still receiving royalties and expenses. He

Photograph by John Miner, dated May 26, 1952. Marian Bruce Logan recalled that Billy would primarily play classical music for her private audience—and jazz only on request.

"TONK" (1940)

By 1940, Ellington had written many concertos for his star soloists, but he had overlooked himself as a candidate for such a feature. Strayhorn took care of that omission with his "Tonk," a striking, dissonant composition that celebrated Ellington's Harlem Stride piano style but at the same time provided a tongue-in-cheek commentary on this (by 1940) somewhat outdated technique.

The band never performed the orchestral version of "Tonk," but the two collaborators performed the work as a four-hand piano piece on several occasions. The *quatre-main* version of "Tonk" could have very well originated from the initial rehearsals in which Strayhorn must have showed Ellington his piano part. Strayhorn did not write the piano part in the score since it was faster, easier, and common "ear cat" practice to rely on show-and-tell rather than on manuscript paper. That Ellington was the student and Strayhorn the composer is also clear in the manuscript itself. Ellington actually added chord symbols to Strayhorn's completed score so that he could keep track of the harmonic progression.

If one takes the date on the score into account—"Tonk" was written between February 1940 and November 1940—it becomes clear what a tremendous asset Strayhorn was to the Ellington organization. After barely a year with the band, he was already stretching the orchestra's musical boundaries and redefining the art of composing for the jazz orchestra. "Tonk" may not

have found its way into the Ellington repertoire, but a number of the work's musical ideas definitely did.

—*Walter van de Leur*

RECOMMENDED RECORDING

○ Dutch Jazz Orchestra, *Portrait of a Silk Thread: Newly Discovered Works of Billy Strayhorn* (Challenge 1995)

ABOVE: This record features the best known of the versions of "Tonk," laid down in November 1950. (The original was for big band, 1940.) The duets of the October/November Mercer sessions were later combined with the Pettiford sessions in an album by Riverside, *Great Times*.

AARON BRIDGERS

PIANIST, FRIEND, AND PARTNER

Music, music, music—music was everything to him. When we lived together in New York [in the early 1940s], he used to sit at the table studying scores. He had scores by Stravinsky and Bartok—symphonies and ballets. He was fascinated by how these composers combined folk music and classical music, and he had in his mind to do the same kind of thing with Ellington.

His concentration was total. One time, he was studying music, and I had the radio on, and so I turned it off. He said, "No, leave it on." He wasn't bothered by anything around him. He could turn off the world. I could be playing the piano or playing a record, and he could be writing a piece of music at the same time. His concentration was fabulous. He heard his music in his head when he was writing, and all he had to do was write it down. He knew exactly how it sounded before he wrote it down.

His concentration was so great that it was like he was meditating. I used to look at him and say, "You look like Buddha." He wrote a song based on that, but he spelled it funny [as "Boo-Dah."] He had great wisdom, like Buddha, also. He would say things that explained everything in a few words—"That's not the truth." "Stop that—that will hurt you." He used to say things, and I'd say to him, "Where did you come from? Who are you?"

He loved life, and he lived very, very well. I don't know where he got the money, if Duke paid the bills or what, but he did whatever he wanted. He'd hire a limousine to take a ride through Central Park. I'd try to make him economize sometimes, and he'd say, "No—you only live once."

After I moved to Paris, he came to visit me quite often. There were several places he'd always go. He'd always go shopping. He'd go to Westin's and buy six or eight pairs of shoes, and their shoes were very expensive shoes. He'd buy a beautiful pair of shoes in black, and he'd ask, "Do you have them in brown, too?" One time, he bought beautiful gloves for the wives of every member of the Duke Ellington Orchestra. He was a fantastic gift giver.

I'd ask him, "How are you paying for all of this?" And he'd just smile.

Very shortly after he died, I was playing piano at a place called the Living Room [in Paris]. I was the house pianist. One night, Ava Gardner came in with a party, and she came up to the piano to talk to me, because she knew that Billy and I used to live together. She asked me to play "Lush Life," and she said, "How is that dear boy of yours?"

I told her that he had passed, and she let out a terrible scream. The room fell silent like there was a murder or something going on. She put her arms around me and held me. She just held me. She wouldn't let me go.

As told to David Hajdu

He loved life, and he lived very, very well. . . .
I'd try to make him economize sometimes, and he'd say,
"No—you only live once."

"HE HEARD HIS MUSIC IN HIS HEAD WHEN HE WAS WRITING, AND ALL HE HAD TO DO WAS WRITE IT DOWN. HE KNEW EXACTLY HOW IT SOUNDED BEFORE HE WROTE IT DOWN."

—AARON BRIDGERS

Strayhorn and Billy Eckstine seated at piano with two men behind them, circa 1958. Photograph by Charles "Teenie" Harris, American, 1908–1998, Kodak Safety Film, H: 4 in. x W: 5 in., Carnegie Museum of Art, Pittsburgh, Heinz Family Fund.

would occasionally complete work Duke would send over. According to the Henderson interview in Hajdu's biography, Duke called him the next day declaring that he (Henderson) did not need Billy because his talent surpassed Strayhorn's. Luther never discussed the conversation with Billy, but somehow both men drew back and let the project die. They never picked up *Rose-Colored Glasses* again.

Despite their failure to launch the play, a number of songs survive, including "Love Has Passed Me By Again," recorded on the Dutch Jazz Orchestra's CDs. Here are a handful of lyrics from the tune:

Love has passed me by again
Don't ask me why
I simply cannot tell you
How love could pass me by again
And cast me in the role of Romeo at large

I have lived life placidly
Passing flames have lasted me
But no great love has blasted me to the heights
I guess I have missed my cue again
There's still no you to make my life worth living
It seems that love has passed me by again
I have traveled far and wide
Cupid's cavalry to ride
But there's only gravel deep inside my soul
I guess I'll go find those blues again
The sad conclusion to my tale of woe
Is simply love has passed me by again

The late Maya Angelou recorded a reading of Strayhorn lyrics because of their poetic value. Many of Billy's songs deal with melancholy. Clearly they mirrored his own strivings to find meaning in his personal life.

LINER NOTES

"AFTER ALL" (1941)

The first three notes of its languid theme fit the title, and that was about as much as Strayhorn was willing to share about this composition. The song provides precious little insight into what inspired the composer to write the piece. "After All" is one of those seemingly simple pieces that Strayhorn could write without any effort. But don't be fooled: the theme moves through some surprisingly modernist chords. Strayhorn wrote it at a time when Ellington suddenly needed a new repertoire, as the 1941 broadcasting ban had blacked out the orchestra's regular band book. Only a couple of performances during the Second World War years are documented, after which the song was abandoned.

But the song's absence from the orchestra's studio work does not necessarily mean Strayhorn lost interest in it. In the mid-1950s, he made a remarkable new arrangement, which ended up on *And His Mother Called Him Bill*. In its new guise as a full feature for Johnny Hodges's alto, the song proved its vitality and continues to grow in popularity.

—Walter van de Leur

RECOMMENDED RECORDING

◉ Ken Peplowski, *Upper Manhattan Medical Group: Remembering Billy Strayhorn* (Mainstern 2007)

OPPOSITE: Ellington shares his traditional four kisses with Billy. In 1971 when President Nixon observed the Duke's practice, he asked him, "Why four kisses?" "One for each cheek, Mr. President."

During this time period, Billy would travel with Lena as her pianist. He accompanied her on piano for fourteen recordings made under Lennie Hayton's supervision for RCA. One tune that he composed specifically for Lena's voice is titled "Maybe."

REEVALUATING ELLINGTON/STRAYHORN

In late 1955 Billy had been in Paris for over a month, returning to New York the second week of the new year. It was to be a new era for Strayhorn and Ellington. Duke set Billy free to do a hot project with the very popular singer Rosemary Clooney. The Ellington band recorded a set of Billy's arrangements in New York. Then he flew to Los Angeles, where he coached and supervised Ms. Clooney in overdubbing the vocals—a relatively new process for the era.

Strayhorn found solace from the stresses of working for Ellington by travel, often to Paris "to ease the bite of it"—sometimes for work, more often for reunions with Aaron Bridgers.

Next came the Newport Jazz Festival, which was an important event with jazz having fallen from the pop mainstream. Strayhorn's contributions helped to make the festival a smashing success. Columbia Records released *Ellington at Newport* shortly thereafter to rave reviews. The Ellington band was truly back and riding the crest of a new wave of excitement in this post–big band era. Ellington appeared on the cover of *Time* magazine for a six-page story. According to Van de Leur, Strayhorn wrote two-thirds of the *Newport Jazz Festival Suite*. Reunited in a new way, Billy and Duke agreed to have dinner together. This was the first time they had ever discussed their collaborative relationship in terms of negotiations. Duke proposed a toast to their new incorporation. To define this incorporation, Ellington is quoted in Hajdu's biography, "I need you. From now on, your name is up there, right next to mine. It's Duke Ellington and Billy Strayhorn." The string of musical pearls resulting from this collaboration has never been equaled before or since.

1. A television world premiere of the musical *A Drum Is a Woman* performed on *The United States Steel Hour.* (1957)
2. The musical recording *Such Sweet Thunder.* (1957)
3. The sound track for the Otto Preminger movie *Anatomy of a Murder*, starring James Stewart, Lee Remick, and Ben Gazzara. (1959)

"JUST A-SITTIN' AND A-ROCKIN'" (1941)

The instrumental original "Just A-Settin' and A-Rockin'" was recorded in 1941 but copyrighted in 1944 as "Just A-Sittin' and A-Rockin'" (note the one-letter difference!) after Delta Rhythm Boys member Lee Gaines wrote lyrics to the tune. (He is also credited as the lyricist for "Take the 'A' Train.") Strayhorn held on to the original title—his 1950s score for the session with Rosemary Clooney is titled "Settin' + Rockin'." The piece is credited to both Ellington and Strayhorn, and here, it is difficult to positively establish who wrote what since

the original score is missing. There are, however, a number of early, untitled sketches in Strayhorn's hand, and the inclusion of the work on *The Peaceful Side* might hint at the original composer, too.

—Walter van de Leur

RECOMMENDED RECORDING

⊙ Billy Strayhorn & The Paris String Quartet, *The Peaceful Side* (Capitol 1961)

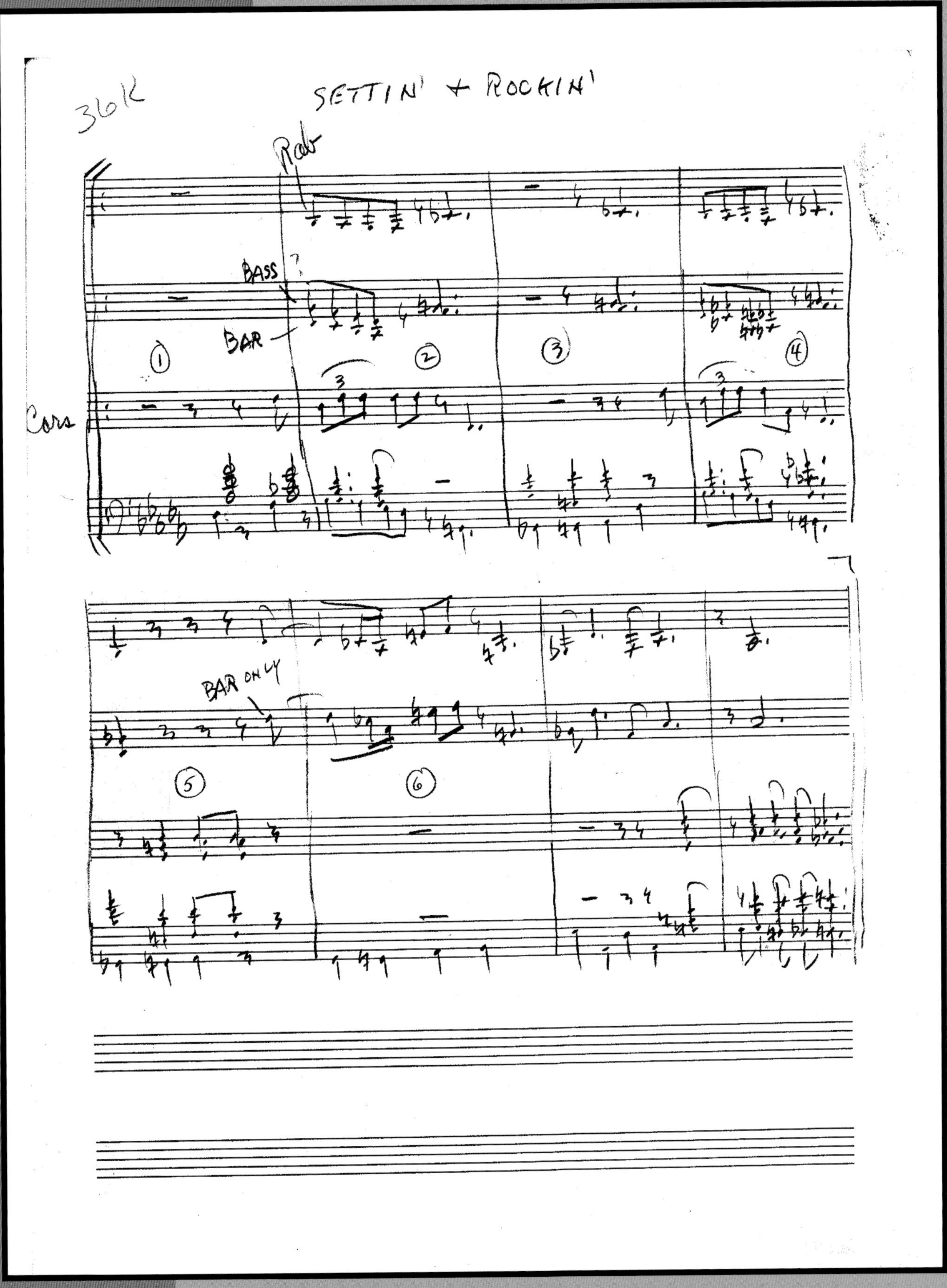
36K
SETTIN' + ROCKIN'
BASS
BAR
Cors
BAR ONLY
1
2
3
4
5
6

4. The groundbreaking adaptation of Tchaikovsky's *The Nutcracker Suite* arranged in the jazz idiom (1960) and Edvard Grieg's *Peer Gynt Suite*. (1960)
5. The movie sound track for the Martin Ritt film *Paris Blues*, starring Sidney Poitier and Paul Newman. (1961)

This unprecedented flow of music highlights the illustrious career of a true genius. Billy was able to not only write enduring songs, but he also composed enduring jazz compositions. Only a select few have accomplished this feat.

Unfortunately, in addition to his gifts, Billy also had a number of demons and challenges that negatively impacted him. His abuse of alcohol and tobacco most certainly contributed to his death at age fifty-one from esophageal cancer. He was also not very astute about the business of his music making, which made him vulnerable to the subordination of his legacy both in history and in real life.

His openly gay lifestyle harmed him because the jazz world was very macho and antigay. Then the real blow came in 1965 when he was diagnosed with esophageal cancer. The final two years of his life were filled with suffering. Many times I sat vigil with my uncle. He was so full of medication that he wasn't always lucid. We answered the telephone for him. Nevertheless, he faced his death with dignity

STRAYHORN'S FIRST GLIMPSES OF NEW YORK

Aaron Bridgers (Pianist and Strayhorn's Partner): Duke Ellington lived on Edgecombe Avenue in Harlem's Sugar Hill neighborhood. Duke's son, Mercer, and his sister, Ruth Ellington, had this huge apartment with very expensive furniture. It was really quite fabulous.

Lillian Strayhorn: The furniture was arranged along a wall like a V. The color scheme was gray and pink, and even the books had gray covers. It was very posh. There was a beautiful portrait of Duke's mother hanging on the wall, and the corner table had what I thought was a real plant growing inside of it. At age ten, this was simply fascinating—I was thinking, "Wow, I was in high cotton!"

AB: Mercer showed me around New York. And one day, I was sitting on a park bench, and Mercer brought this guy over and said, "Aaron Bridgers, meet Billy Strayhorn." And Billy said, "Pleased to meet you." We found that we had a lot of things in common.

He told me that Ellington had hired him in Pittsburgh as a lyricist, but he hadn't had a chance at that time to show him his musical compositions. At that time Duke was touring Europe, so I took Billy down to hear Art Tatum. We used to go out quite often and always stayed out very late. Bars didn't close until 4 o'clock in the morning back then.

Jean Bach (Colleague and Publicist): Duke told me, "I've met this young fellow who is very fond of our band." He said, "We'll keep him for a year, and then we'll send him out in the world, and he'll be our protégé!" Ellington said, "Now, Jean, I would like you to design some things for his graduation ceremony."

Duke wanted me to design the costumes that he and Billy Strayhorn were supposed to wear at this so-called farewell ceremony. He said, "Now, cap and gowns, and think of some interesting color. The costumes will be one thing," he said, "but what's also very important is the diploma. Now I'm going to present him with a diploma, so can you please work on that too?"

—Robert Levi

DUKE ELLINGTON, INC.
333 Riverside Drive
New York, New York 10025

BILLY STRAYHORN

Poor little Sweet Pea, Billy Strayhorn, William Thomas Strayhorn the biggest human being who ever lived, a man with the greatest courage, the most majestic artistic statue, a highly skilled musician whose impeccable taste commanded the respect of all musicians and the admiration of all listeners.

His audiences at home and abroad marvelled at the grandeur of his talent and the mantle of tonal supremacy that he wore only with grace. He was a beautiful human being, adored by a wide range of friends, rich, poor, famous and unknown. Great artists pay homage to Billy Strayhorn's mastery of his craft. Because of his God-given creative ability - because of applying himself to his rare sensitivity, Billy Strayhorn accomplished a marriage of melody, words and harmony like fitting made compatible with happiness.

Billy Strayhorn's greatest virtue, I think, was his honesty, not only to others, but to himself. His listening-hearing self was totally intolerant of his writing-playing self, when or if any compromise was expected or considered expedient. Condescension did not exist in the mind of Billy Strayhorn.

Billy Strayhorn spoke English perfectly and Frency very well. He demanded freedom of expression and lived what we consider the most important and moral freedoms. Freedom from hate, unconditionally, freedom from all self-pity (even throughout all the pain and bad news), freedom from fear of possibly doing something that might help himself more than it would help another, and freedom from the kind of pride that could make a man feel he was better than his brother or neighbor.

His patience incomparable and unlimited with no aspirations to enter into any kind of competition, but in spite of it all, that which will constitute his oeuvre, will never be less than the ultimate on the highest plateau of culture, (whether by comparison or not). GOD BLESS BILLY STRAYHORN

DUKE ELLINGTON
May 31, 1967

and resolve. He wrote his last song on his deathbed: "Blood Count." Today "Blood Count" is one of the most recorded and performed Strayhorn pieces by the up-coming jazz generation. Billy died on May 31, 1967.

At Strayhorn's memorial, Ellington read comments that he had composed upon first hearing the news of Strayhorn's death, alluding again to the moral freedoms he described upon accepting the Medal of Freedom from President Nixon (see p. 77).

Ellington recorded a tribute album to Strayhorn, *And His Mother Called Him Bill*, which won a Grammy Award in 1968. Many say it was his best album. One of the tracks is unedited—after the session was over, Ellington remained in the studio alone and was captured tearfully playing his favorite Strayhorn song, "Lotus Blossom."

OPPOSITE: Carl Van Vechten knew many of the figures of the Harlem Renaissance. His ongoing interest in African American musicians led to a series of photographs of Billy made on August 19, 1958.

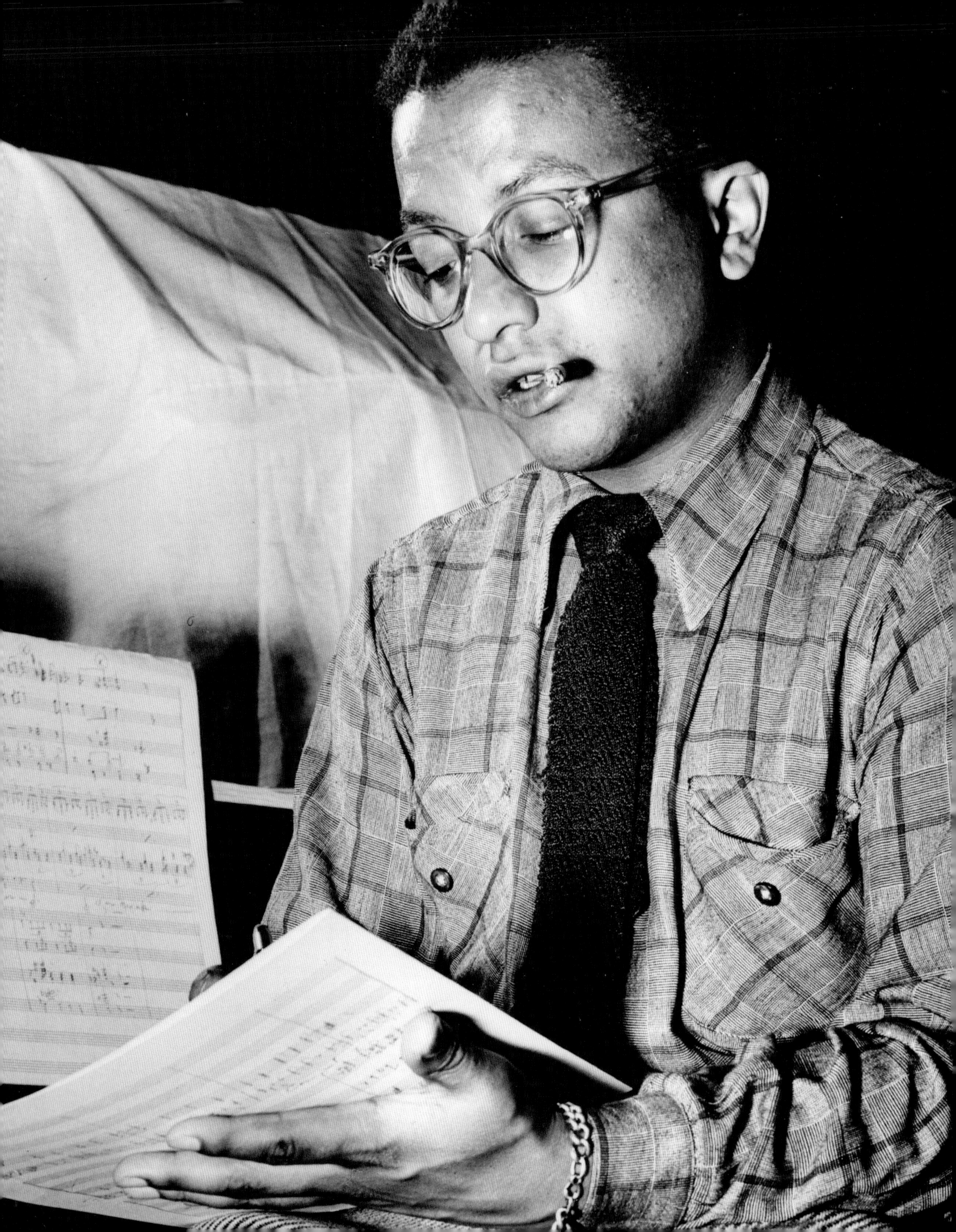

MORAL FREEDOMS

The path to success was not an easy one for Billy Strayhorn, and yet he marched it with grace and genius. Even though the times in which he lived presented no end of obstacles and constraints, Strayhorn clung to his ideals and moral freedoms and succeeded not only musically but also culturally and socially.

Young Billy in school. He is in the second row, far right.

CIVIL RIGHTS ACTIVIST

As a child Billy Strayhorn was presented with daunting challenges—illness, poverty, an abusive, alcoholic father, and always and everywhere, racial discrimination. After his birth and first five years in Dayton, his father's "plain ole wanderlust" caused Billy to spend "the rest of my little years see-sawing"[2] between New Jersey, North Carolina, and the Pittsburgh suburbs of Braddock and Rankin before finally landing in Homewood. Billy's sister Lillian described the family's adopted home as a "hard scrabble town."[3] It was not the worst place to grow up in the segregation era, but it presented more than enough obstacles to its black youth.

Roots in the Burgh

The often-detailed story of white orchestra teacher Carl McVicker's encouragement of Strayhorn's high school accomplishments must be seen in the larger context of the school's repressive atmosphere. It was integrated, with black students comprising 12 percent of Billy's graduating class (17 of 145), but opportunities were not equal for all students. There were no black teachers in any Pittsburgh public school. Students of color were forbidden from participating in the WHS orchestra or working on the staff of school publications. They were denied membership in the lily-white Etiquette Club, the Penn Club, and other extracurricular organizations. School textbooks were full of racial stereotypes. Black students were regularly required to sing songs in which they were depicted as slaves and menials.

Sophia Bailey Nelson, mother of five, fought to change those inequities for her children and their

7212 Tioga Street Rear in the Homewood district of Pittsburgh, the home of the Strayhorns during Billy's youth. In the mixed-race neighborhood, better-off families lived in homes that faced the street; poorer families lived off the alley to the rear of the address.

LINER NOTES

"CHELSEA BRIDGE" (1941)

"Chelsea Bridge" was reportedly inspired by one of James Abbott McNeill Whistler's hazy, dark-toned paintings of London's Chelsea Embankment. With its subdued orchestral colors, the piece also bespeaks Strayhorn's fondness for the compositions of Claude Debussy, who once described his own *Nocturnes* as "an experiment in the different combinations that can be achieved with one color—what a study in gray would be in painting." That description strikingly fits both Whistler's London paintings and Strayhorn's "Chelsea Bridge." More French influences can be found in the theme's opening bars, which echo the second movement of Maurice Ravel's piano piece *Valses Nobles et Sentimentales*. Still, much as Strayhorn alludes to these so-called French impressionists, "Chelsea Bridge" is entirely original. By blending turn-of-the-century European elements into an otherwise African American idiom, he went beyond a mere imitation of his influences. Not surprisingly, his contemporaries were deeply impressed, including composer-arranger Gil Evans, who later worked with Miles Davis on some of his best-known records. Evans said, "From the moment I first heard 'Chelsea Bridge,' I set out to try to do that. That's all I did—that's all I ever did—try to do what Billy Strayhorn did."

—*Walter van de Leur*

RECOMMENDED RECORDING

○ Ben Webster, *Music for Loving: Ben Webster with Strings* (Verve 1955)

"FROM THE MOMENT I FIRST HEARD 'CHELSEA BRIDGE,' I SET OUT TO TRY TO DO THAT. THAT'S ALL I DID—THAT'S ALL I EVER DID—TRY TO DO WHAT BILLY STRAYHORN DID."

—GIL EVANS

WHS French Club, Billy's senior year (1933–1934). He is center right in the photograph.

Young Billy at the piano. He played Grieg's *Piano Concerto in A Minor* at Westinghouse High School on March 1, 1934.

classmates. She mentored James Miller and Lawrence Peeler, who became the first black members of the WHS orchestra.[4] From a reluctant administration she won equal membership opportunities in clubs and organizations for qualified black pupils. She joined the NAACP, formed its Youth Council in Pittsburgh, and taught "Negro History" and racial pride to her students. Later, as the first NAACP Pennsylvania State Conference President (1942–1944), she fought to accomplish hiring of black teachers and created door-to-door voter registration drives in African American neighborhoods.

Billy's time at WHS was coincident with that of the two youngest Nelson children. Sophia Phillips Nelson was secretary of Strayhorn's beloved *Le cercle*

"RAIN CHECK" (1941)

During the first weeks of 1941, the Ellington orchestra was booked for an extensive engagement at the Casa Mañana in Culver City, a venue with a radio wire. But shortly before the band settled on the West Coast, a conflict over licensing fees between the American Society of Composers, Authors and Publishers (ASCAP) and the radio networks exploded. The resulting broadcasting ban virtually blacked out all ASCAP-controlled music for the larger part of the year. Ellington was an ASCAP member, and he consequently saw his repertoire blocked from the airwaves. It was a chance opportunity for Strayhorn, who swiftly came up with new songs for the orchestra, including some of his most famous works, "Take the 'A' Train," "Chelsea Bridge," and "Rain Check."

"That was about rain, about being in California. . . . I was sitting at home in Los Angeles, and writing," Strayhorn said when asked what inspired "Rain Check." As Mark Tucker pointed out, "For Strayhorn, looking back, the piece was linked to no program or picture other than the compositional process itself, and the specific circumstances under which the work was undertaken." "Rain Check" solidly swings, while providing a multitude of colors and moods—many more than a Californian rainstorm will ever create.

—Walter van de Leur

RECOMMENDED RECORDING

○ Marian McPartland, *Marian McPartland Plays the Music of Billy Strayhorn* (Concord 1992)

Français; she was editor of the school paper, *Bulletin*, and valedictorian of Billy's January 1934 class (when she was just fifteen years old). Fannetta, twenty-two months younger than Sophia, born on Billy's fourth birthday and like him a precocious pianist, sat second chair to Strayhorn in the select Orchestra Club. They were the only two black students to play in the prestigious ensemble during Strayhorn's time at WHS.[5]

Extreme institutionalized prejudice at Westinghouse High School is epitomized by racist principal Clark Benjamin Kistler, who said after Sophia's achievement, "There will never be another—the word was not Negro—valedictorian on his watch."[6] Two years later, when Fannetta also won the distinction, Kistler threatened enlightened conductor McVicker with termination of his job if he did not lower Fannetta's music grades from A to B. McVicker caved.[7]

In spite of imposed racial limitations at WHS, Billy carved out a place for himself. He was selected to the Penn Club in his sophomore year, providing an opportunity to hone his creative writing proclivities.[8] In his senior year he became the club's president. He also rose to the top of the school's musical establishment, playing the Grieg *Piano Concerto* with the Orchestra Club at his graduation and presenting his own *Concerto for Piano and Percussion* with white classmate Mickey Scrima. His duets with Harry Herforth (trumpeter) were presented in school assemblies, PTA meetings, and even before the city Board of Education. Herforth recalled, "I don't know how many of the people who heard us were expecting a mixed-race duo, but we certainly were subjected to a lot of glares. I do think it softened the blow that Billy was perceived as my accompanist, though that's not at all how we wanted to be seen."[9]

HERB JEFFRIES

SINGER, DUKE ELLINGTON ORCHESTRA

Strayhorn and I hit it off right away. First of all, we were the youngest people in the band, so we had something in common. And not only that, but I had French in school and was fair with it and Strayhorn was highly skilled at French, you know. He spoke French very well, and so of course that fascinated me. We had this little thing in the band that nobody else had: we could talk and nobody could understand what we were talking about. So we spoke to each other in French. We were in a different strata than the other guys in the band.

In those days, it always gave you a little bit of an edge if here you are a black man sitting in some place speaking French. Remember, in those days there was a tremendous amount of discrimination, and, of course, you could show a certain amount of sophistication by the mere fact that you could speak a language that some redneck or somebody else couldn't. That meant you weren't that lowly person, that Amos and Andy character that everybody thought you were.

Strayhorn had that same feeling about that that I did. He wanted to show that there was some dignity in all races of people.

Of course, he took a tremendous interest in my voice and wanted to help me develop. When I started traveling with the band, before Strayhorn got a hold of me, I used to sing very high, in a high voice. Backstage, I used to clown around and do some imitations. So one night I was someplace—I forget where it was, down south—and I was imitating Bing Crosby, and when Strayhorn heard that he said, "Oh, I like you in that lower register. That's great. That's the voice I want."

So Strayhorn said to Duke, "That's the voice I want for him." And they brought me all the way down from a very high voice into that mellow voice. It was Strayhorn who did it. He changed my life as a singer. I admired him greatly, and I loved him very, very much.

As told to David Hajdu

Billy was invited to return to WHS the year following his graduation: for the Stunt Day production of his Gershwinesque review *Fantastic Rhythm* (later given at a string of other Pittsburgh high schools and in black theaters throughout southwestern Pennsylvania) and to play his arrangement of Rimsky-Korsakov's "Song of India" with graduating senior Jerome Eisner, clarinetist.

His impressive musical activities won him a scholarship "in music to any institution of his choice,"[10] though that was hardly how things worked. Post-secondary educational opportunities were specifically stratified for musicians—black collegians were advised in clear terms that dreams of a solo classical career were futile: they *could* study jazz or education, though the Pittsburgh Public Schools did not *hire* black teachers; outside the academy, integrated small ensembles of classical musicians (like Herforth/Strayhorn; Eisner/Strayhorn) either did not exist or were not allowed to for long—there was simply no work. Equal opportunity for black musicians in professional orchestra auditions was decades away. Billy persisted. He enrolled in

Throughout his career, Strayhorn would visit family in Pittsburgh for special occasions and holidays. He remained particularly close with Robert "Bobby" Conaway, who served as his rehearsal pianist during the production of *Fantastic Rhythm*. Conaway married Billy's sister Georgia and they had six children and lived in a small sequestered housing development in Glen Hazel. Christmas holidays were particularly special because Billy would return home and sometimes stay with the Conaways, bringing gifts and sharing piano duets with Conaway. In those days, getting from New York to Pittsburgh by plane could take four hours, and it was often necessary to arrive at a late hour. The Conaways would be asleep for the night but would leave the front door unlocked so that Billy could come inside. He did so and would go straight for the piano and begin loudly playing, waking everyone up. The kids would jump excitedly out of bed exclaiming, "Uncle Billy is here!" and then everyone would run downstairs to greet him. Billy kept similar relationships with his other Pittsburgh relatives.

"JOHNNY COME LATELY" (1942)

Late in 1939, a new double bass player joined the Duke Ellington Orchestra: Jimmie Blanton. In his short stay with the band, he revolutionized the approach to the instrument. Where bass players tended to play with a steady, thud-like sound, Blanton played intricate and clearly audible lines and at times soloed in a fashion that later became the model for future bassists. Charles Mingus, for one, carefully transcribed Blanton's playing from records, as his papers reveal.

Some of the parts that Strayhorn wrote for Blanton are titled "Moe," which may have been a nickname. It was customary in the band to personalize parts: the parts for Hodges (nicknamed "Rabbit") were made out to Rab rather than to alto. The original autograph for "Johnny Come Lately" is titled "Moe" as well, which makes one think that there might be a connection. Is "Johnny Come Lately" by any chance dedicated to Blanton, who was in the hospital with tuberculosis at the time the piece was written? As with so many titles in Strayhorn's oeuvre, we shall never know what exactly he had in mind. Blanton, who was anything but a Johnny-come-lately, passed away a month after the piece was first recorded.

—Walter van de Leur

RECOMMENDED RECORDING

○ Joe Henderson, *Lush Life: The Music of Billy Strayhorn* (Verve 1992)

ABOVE: More duets featuring Strays and Duke were recorded in November, this time with Joe Shulman as bassist. Prestige Records bought a significant portion of the Sunrise and Mercer catalog after those companies folded.

BILLY STRAYHORN GROWS INTO THE PART

It didn't take long for Strayhorn to assimilate to the fashionable world of jazz and cocktails that he described in "Lush Life," a classic and timeless composition that he wrote in Pittsburgh when he was sixteen years old.

Gerald Wilson (Composer, Bandleader, and Trumpeter): I met Billy Strayhorn in 1941 in New York City. He would show me things on the piano that he could do, and he'd say, "Gerald, you can do this, too. Try it like this." Billy had total command of the instrument. And with the harmonic ability he had, he could do things that were fantastic. He knew so much about music that I assumed he'd had years and years of training. He must have practiced, practiced, practiced.

Don Shirley (Pianist, Bandleader, and Composer): Duke and Billy hit it off, and it was right that they did. They had deep regard and respect for one another. They thought along the same lines because they were both rebels.

David Baker (Composer and Bandleader): Billy had a wonderful technique and touch. If you listen to him on the piano duets with Ellington, you can hear how beautifully he plays the instrument, but it's more akin to what I'd expect to hear from someone who studied the music of Chopin or Schubert, because it's such a refined way of playing.

Jean Bach: Ivie Anderson, who was the band's vocalist during that time, took to Billy right away. One of my earliest memories of Billy was he and I having dinner with Ivie. Billy looked over the menu—and he was already showing signs of his later enthusiasm for France—and there was an item that said, "Rissolé potatoes." Billy said, "Now what could that be?"

I took a million years of French in school but had no idea what it meant. And now Billy's mind is working on it. He said, "Could it mean 'resolved' potatoes? One of these days, I must look it up in a cookbook to see what it actually is." But he had that kind of intense curiosity back then.

Mercedes Ellington (Granddaughter of Duke Ellington): Billy Strayhorn's wit, sharp mindedness, and the search for the new, the unexpected, and the unexplored were typical of the world that Billy lived in. There's an intellect there that knows no match. And he had such a taste for clothing—when you look at pictures of Billy, it's as if he knew that somebody was taking photos of him, and he was never caught unaware.

—Robert Levi

---

the only collegiate program in Pittsburgh that allowed black students to major in performance—the Pittsburgh Musical Institute. He attracted the interest of cofounder and internationally known scholar Charles Newell Boyd and began advanced studies in fall 1936. On April 24, 1937, Boyd suddenly died while playing religious music for a Pittsburgh pastor at the Institute. Billy left school believing there was no one else there wonderful enough to teach him.[11]

Through the influence of drummer Mickey Scrima and another white friend, guitarist Bill Esch, Strayhorn's interest soon gravitated to jazz piano. He set out on the typical path of jazz education at his time—finding an individual playing style based on those of his favored models: Tatum, Hines, and Wilson, with a hefty bit of influence from Rachmaninoff, Debussy, and Ravel.

Eschewing the more numerous race clubs on the Hill, he found solo gigs in the establishments of white East Liberty "because they attracted the more legitimate musicians and wealthier patrons—they represented success and prominence."[12] One such venue on Apple Street was owned by Woogie Harris and was a gathering place for players in the Musicians' Protective Union, still segregated groups at this time,

One of Billy's first jobs with the Ellington organization was working with singers. He and Herb Jeffries developed a deep friendship as well. Jeffries said, "He'd work very, very closely with you, and he sensed what your strengths were. Then he picked songs and did the arrangements to bring out the best in you."

"STRANGE FEELING" (1943)

The first collaborative suite that Ellington and Strayhorn wrote was the *Perfume Suite*. It stands as a model for the many suites that followed. Each composer contributed individually written works to these suites. At times, these works were composed for other occasions, but under a new title and accompanied by a good story, they fit a certain suite's theme. The *Perfume Suite* is an excellent case in point because it recycled two Strayhorn works.

The first movement from the suite was an excerpt from Strayhorn's "Pentonsilic" (recorded posthumously by the Dutch Jazz Orchestra), with an introduction from an unrecorded arrangement of Mack Gordon and Harry Warren's 1941 ballad "Where You Are." The second movement originated from an extended engagement

in 1943 at the Hurricane on Broadway in New York. The band accompanied a "new hit revue" titled "Strange Feeling," a floor show that featured dancer Leticia Hill. Strayhorn provided a spooky theme for the show—the original score is titled "Leticia." Retitled as "Violence," the theme was used as the second movement of the 1944 *Perfume Suite*. The original "Strange Feeling" was dear to Strayhorn, as illustrated by its inclusion decades later in *The Peaceful Side* sessions.

—*Walter van de Leur*

RECOMMENDED RECORDING

○ Billy Strayhorn, *The Peaceful Side* (Capitol 1961)

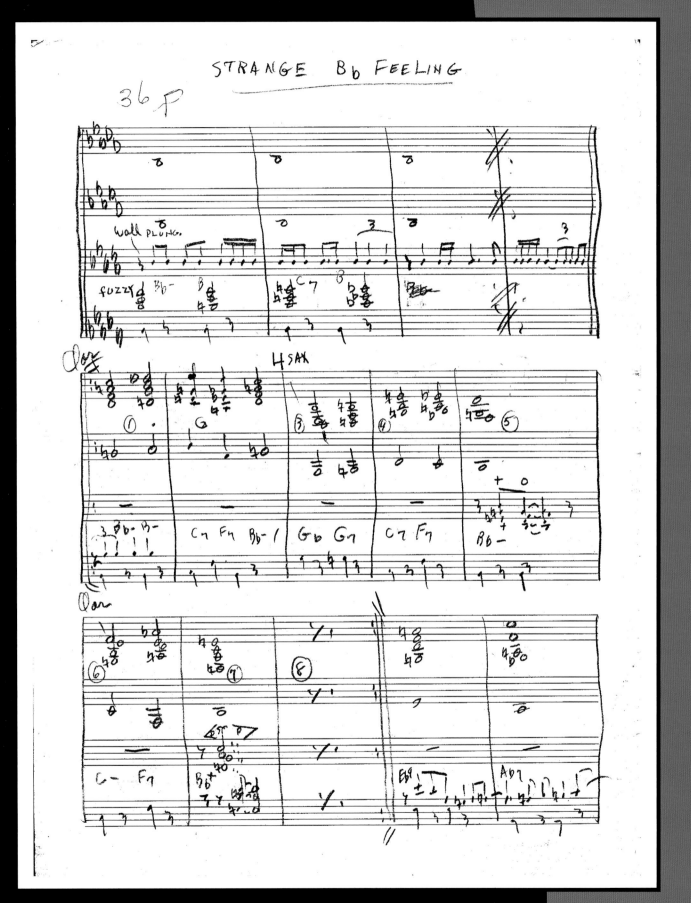

but integrated in their appreciation of performances at the club. Like his piano teacher Charlotte Dyer Enty Catlin and her musical partner Lena Horne,[13] Billy was well paid for performances at parties in private homes of wealthy white society.

He augmented solo work by creating interracial ensembles, virtually unheard of in the '30s. One such group was composed of clarinet partner Eisner and a wealthy white drummer, Calvin Dort. After a year of success at Charlie Ray's, one of the shadier East Liberty joints, and a summer of work at an amusement park at Rakuen Lakes, southwest of Pittsburgh, the group found a six-night-a-week engagement at a new nightclub in Winchester, Virginia. Pressed for a name, Eisner chose Mad Hatters, and the group headed south. Billy slept on a cot in a back room of the club while the two white players had boarding-house accommodations.

Several weeks into their contract, prejudice infiltrated the club when a patron shouted a remark about "that nigger on piano." Dort kicked his drums at the offender, and the trio beat it back to more tolerant land to the north. Eisner recalled the incident made quite the impression on Strayhorn: "It didn't make him give up though—just the opposite. He was even more thoughtful and determined than usual. That's when he started talking about different ways to pursue his music."[14] Mad Hatters made a recording in the studio of Volkwein's Music and then retired.

Billy became involved with larger groups, first as an arranger for the rehearsal band of drummer Bill Ludwig, then for another similar ensemble, the Buddy Malone Orchestra. Because of his flowering reputation with these groups, he was offered a solo position with the newly forming, fifteen-piece Rex Edwards Orchestra. One of only two black players in the group—"absolutely unheard of, to everybody who saw it," Strayhorn improved the 120 stock arrangements in its book, led rehearsals, and performed at

"CHARPOY" (AKA "LANA TURNER") (1944)

Whether Strayhorn's miniature trumpet concerto indeed was dedicated to the blonde Hollywood film star whom he befriended in the early '40s remains unknown, but if so, Strayhorn must have thought highly of her: "Lana Turner" is a beautiful composition, full of rich harmonies, resplendent melodic turns, and warm orchestrations.

Strayhorn kept returning to "Lana Turner" throughout his career, writing new variations on its theme and creating alternate orchestral settings. For instance, a year after he first composed the piece, he wrote another version that he registered for copyright as "Francesca." (That female subject remains unknown.) Decades later, after the Ellingtonians visited the Middle and Near East—a trip that resulted in the Ellington-Strayhorn *Far East Suite*—he rescored the piece again and gave it a more curious moniker: "Charpoy," the Hindi word for *daybed*. The work is best known under that title.

—*Walter van de Leur*

RECOMMENDED RECORDING

◉ Terell Stafford, *This Side of Strayhorn* (MaxJazz 2011)

social functions and private parties throughout 1938.[15]

Events of December 2, 1938, changed it all. The audition with Ellington swept Billy out of hardscrabble Pittsburgh. There he had experienced ugly injustice, and he had learned the necessity of fighting for opportunities to express himself and to be himself, whatever the cost.

billy strayhorn
310 riverside drive
new york, n. y. 10025

Dear Arturo,
a pittance on
account — Love

B

Strayhorn's "Dear Arturo" (Arthur Logan) was physician to many of the Harlem elite between 1934 and his death in 1973. He treated Billy, his "Itty Bitty Buddy," through his final illness. Logan was buried on what would have been Billy's fifty-eighth birthday, November 29, 1973.

Activism Sprouting in New York City

Less than three weeks after Billy arrived in New York, on February 11, 1939, Duke Ellington donated the services of his orchestra for the New York branch's thirty-year anniversary dance of the NAACP. More than five thousand illustrious and powerful black activists and their white allies celebrated in the 369th Regiment Armory in Harlem. Duke was host and master of ceremonies, and the music of his band was broadcast nationally over CBS radio from midnight until 12:30 a.m.

How could his young, newly received associate not be starstruck as the famous appeared as guests of honor or soloists? Ella Fitzgerald, Ivie Anderson, Bill Robinson, Cab Calloway, Clifton Webb, Alberta Hunter, W. C. Handy. Directors and officials of the association with their wives.[16] The influential A. Philip Randolph, president of the Brotherhood of Sleeping Car Porters and Maids, was there. He was to sit for election to the board of the NAACP the following year and continue that work throughout the rest of Billy's life.

Dr. Arthur Courtney Logan was there too. He was one of the first black graduates of the Columbia University College of Physicians and Surgeons (1934).[17] After completing a two-year internship at Harlem Hospital, he was appointed an associate visiting surgeon and was serving in that capacity when he met Duke Ellington in early July 1937. The band was appearing at Loew's State Theatre, three blocks from the Cotton Club, and it was while hanging out at the old haunt that Duke was introduced to Dr. Logan. Marian Bruce Logan reported many years later, "As Arthur told me, and as Edward told me, they fell madly in love with one another from the beginning. Ellington wanted him as his doctor, and he remained his doctor from '37 until he died."[18] He also became Billy's doctor.

The influence of Ellington, Randolph, and Logan led to Billy becoming literally a poster boy for NAACP voter registration campaigns. One advertisement, created in the early '40s, pictured Strayhorn and

Billy and his godson, Warren Arthur "Chip" Logan,
with Francis Goldberg at the Logan home, 1966.

"Brucie Mae" (Marian Bruce Logan) and "Willyam," dear friends.

HONI COLES

DANCER, MEMBER OF THE COPASETICS

I got to know Billy very well through the club we were in together, the Copasetics. We were so close he called me "Father."

The Copasetics formed in the late 1940s in honor of Bill Robinson [the legendary dancer], who invented the word "copasetic." The club was all dancers at first. We invited Billy to join, even though he wasn't a dancer, because we loved him so much and respected him so much. Such a dignified little guy. And so worldly wise. He had exactly the right comment to make on any subject that came up, seemingly. Consequently, we all respected him. We elected him president of the Copasetics. He remained president until his death, and with his death, we retired the title of president. No one could fill his shoes.

The Copasetics used to gather at his home on Riverside Drive on Sunday afternoons. He would play piano, and we would sing and dance. Billy would cook for the whole gang of us—twelve, fifteen people. He loved cooking nearly as much as he loved music. Red beans was one of his specialties. He cooked them in beer. He loved beans, and he loved beer.

He was a complicated man—full of joy and also unhappiness, which he kept inside. He never sought the limelight, and I don't think he wanted the whole responsibility of a band, where you had to do everything. He could come and go as he pleased. He was his own person—his own person. And that person was complicated.

As told to David Hajdu

Shortly after his arrival in New York, Billy became active in the work of the NAACP. He posed with Ellington copyist Thomas Whaley in front of a voting registration drive poster.

Ellington copyist Thomas Whaley in front of a poster enjoining registration as a vote for equality in jobs, pay, and opportunity.

Ellington was not generally known for participation in organized efforts to promote change of racial inequities. In fact, he was often criticized for his subtlety when dealing with discrimination. When he traveled down south, he rented two Pullman cars—providing both sleeping and eating accommodations for his band, avoiding the impact of Jim Crow laws that barred African Americans from equal hotel and restaurant accommodations. He believed the power of his ducal presence and the music he wrote were sufficient contributions toward altering unfairness. Marian Bruce Logan eloquently stated Duke's logic:

> There are many ways in which you can pay your dues to the civil rights movement. I think Ellington's greatest contribution is the fact that he traveled, and his music was accepted and he was accepted, above and beyond being a black person. There are

"MIDRIFF" (1944)

According to the New Grove Dictionary of Jazz, Strayhorn's "ballads are harmonically and structurally among the most sophisticated." Indeed, his fame as a composer is largely based on his ballad writing. Somewhat less known are Strayhorn's swinging numbers, which he created in a steady stream as well. "Take the 'A' Train" is undoubtedly the most famous in that group, but he wrote many more, including "Rain Check," "All Day Long," "Upper Manhattan Medical Group," and "Midriff."

These compositions have remained less familiar for a number of reasons. First of all, they never managed to become hits (such as Glenn Miller's "In the Mood") mainly because they were written when the swing era was well in decline and war audiences were turning their attention to the more romantic pop singers. But the main reason might lie in the fact that Strayhorn's swingers are orchestral works that cannot be reduced to an easily recognizable theme. "Midriff" provides an excellent case in point: it centers on three different themes that in true Fletcher Henderson style create intricate interlocking textures. Add to that the essential orchestral interludes and the integrated closing section, and it becomes clear that such a piece could never reach the average swing-crazed listener: there is too much going on.

While the larger part of the riff pieces from the swing era have disappeared into oblivion, "Midriff" has gradually become a favorite of many big band musicians. It offers exciting section work, some rewarding solo spots, and great ensemble passages. The trombone solo toward the end deserves special mention: as a buildup to the ad-lib solo chorus, Strayhorn wrote a line that sports a true bebop lick. It stands as proof that he was hip to the then-emerging new genre.

—Walter van de Leur

RECOMMENDED RECORDING

○ Esquire's All-Stars feat. Billy Strayhorn, *Esquire's All-Stars* (1945; Broken Audio 2011)

---

some people . . . who do it in a quiet, continual way, and that's what Ellington did all his life. He projected the black idiom, black music, and his blackness and the blackness of his people. . . . You can't just say that Ellington wrote, created, and played for blacks. He played for people. And because of being a black person himself, what came out of him had to be the black experience.[19]

Billy watched; Billy learned. Billy wrote; Billy traveled. His contributions to Duke's civil rights shows *Jump for Joy* (1941 and 1959), *Beggar's Holiday* (1947), and *A Drum Is a Woman* (1956) have been detailed in Walter van de Leur's book.[20] For the six Carnegie Hall concerts (1943–1948) Ellington programmed pieces reflective of black culture with an eye to impressing the concert-going elite with their sophistication. He drew on Billy for new compositions (with appropriate attribution), but he also attributed pieces to himself that Billy wrote. A third group of pieces was fresh arrangements of Ellington standards and those of other composers (usually without attribution to Billy). The Duke understood Billy's writing helped him accomplish the goals of his subtle activism.

Musical paths of Marian Bruce [later Logan] crossed those of Billy Strayhorn several times before the two

In 1963 Strayhorn became godfather to the Logans' son, Warren Arthur "Chip." Martin Luther King Jr. officiated at the baptism. Rachel Robinson (wife of Jackie), Marguerite Gill, and Dick Thomas were other godparents.

developed a deep personal relationship. Dubbed "tall, tan and terrific" and "the curvaceous lush thrush" by the New York Age newspaper (July 9, 1949; April 9, 1949), Bruce arrived from her native Philadelphia on New Year's Eve in 1945. In truly bizarre fashion she was plucked from her table at Café Society Downtown by former Lena Horne pianist Phil Moore who reasoned, "If she can look like that she can sing" (New York Age, July 9, 1949). Bruce moved to Europe in 1953, enhancing her career but also escaping racism she found on the US performance circuit. Upon her return to the States

she became the nightly dinner companion of Dr. Arthur Logan, who was in a troubled second marriage. According to Jet magazine (October 20, 1955), he was "her constant escort." Bruce continued her career, recording an album with the Luther Henderson Sextet and singer Ozzie Bailey in 1956.

On July 29, 1957, Ellington trumpeter and Strayhorn close friend Clark Terry invited Bruce to Reeves Sound Studios in New York to record Duke's "In a Sentimental Mood" for his album Duke with a Difference. Billy played piano (Luther Henderson, celeste) in a fresh

GUESTS

DATE	NAME	ADDRESS	
11/17/62	AARON R. Bridgrs	24 Rue XAVIER PRIVAS	PARIS 5 FRANCE tel- MED-1422
11-17-62	Leonard A. Weeks	410 CENTRAL PARK W. N.YC.	"Boss"
12/16/62	Bill Grove	410 C. P. W. nyc 25	
11-17-62	Eleanor + Richard Jones	2225 5th Ave. N.Y.C.	"Enchantée"
1/4/62	Billy Strayhorn	310 Riverside Drive	♪ 4 ! ! ♪ ♪ Billy
1/8/62	Anne Lanigan	135 E. 63 St.	Love to the Logans
1/8/63	JIM SHANNON	244 E. 48TH ST.	IT SWINGS — REALLY!
1/8/63	Anne E. Carr	399 W. 72nd Street	C'est magnifique (?)
1/8/63	Frank Reid	145-5th Ave	"Wonderful People"
1/9/63	Tommy Townsend	625 Hanley Way L.A. Calif	"ANGUE"
1/23/63	Harold Hoffman	8131 San Cristobal, Dallas	There's no question, I consent
1/23/63	Harold Edwards	420 E. 72nd St. N.Y.	"I've NEVER had the most wonderful ... like this"

❧

Marian Bruce Logan was frequently kidded for her ubiquitous Instamatics and guest books. This arbitrary page records visits by Aaron Bridgers, Bill Grove, Billy Strayhorn, and Irving Townsend among others. Her archive records the intimate history of her friendships and activism—golden times in Billy's life.

Strayhorn arrangement of the Ellington standard. Billy also provided score and piano solo for "Come Sunday" from *Black, Brown and Beige*.

In March of 1958 Arthur Logan "secured severance papers" from wife Gwen Durham in Mexico and married Bruce on March 28 (*Jet*, March 20, 1958). One last recording fling late in the year included Billy's "Something to Live For." The album title *Halfway to Dawn* came from the late-night, into-the-morning conversations the new friends shared.

He said he liked the fact that it was a kind of in-between state. It wasn't day and it wasn't night. What day was it? You're half asleep. You're half awake. Your resistance is gone—it's like a truth serum. Your feelings just pour out. You don't even realize what you're saying. He loved that, loved it.[21]

Though she loved to contribute a song in social settings, Marian would soon exchange her songbird career for civil rights activism. Billy was her tutor.

BILLY STRAYHORN AND THE BLANTON-WEBSTER ERA

As a new but invaluable member of the Ellington orchestra, Strayhorn helped to engineer the transition into a new, dynamic era of jazz. His compositions fueled a period of prolific creativity known as the "Blanton-Webster Band," named for the innovative bassist Jimmie Blanton and the saxophonist Ben Webster.

Walter van de Leur: Strayhorn is new to the orchestra and so full of ideas that he writes much more than they can possibly record, so some of the rediscovered works—pieces that were shelved—stem from that era. I think there are over one hundred real masterpieces that he wrote in those two years that never saw the recording studio.

Herb Jeffries (Ellington Orchestra Vocalist): Billy had a great effect on Ellington. All of a sudden, Ellington's swing era band became what we call the "Blanton-Webster Band." So it must have had an effect on Duke Ellington for him to even allow that period to be publicized as such. And it was.

Strayhorn's attention to the nuances and strengths of the band's soloists reflected his unique ability to "voice" different talents. No story about Billy Strayhorn could be complete without mentioning his collaboration with tenor saxophonist Ben Webster.

Billy Taylor (Pianist and Bandleader): Ben Webster was a huge man. He played in a dominant way with this enormous, warm sound. To see him with Billy Strayhorn was interesting. I was working with Ben, and Billy came to the Three Deuces to hear him. They started talking—I'd never met Strayhorn at that point—and Strays was joking with Ben about personal experiences between them. It was obvious that this big guy and this little guy really liked each other. I had no idea what they were talking about, but they were in heaven. You didn't get the joke, but what they were doing in the back of this tiny club, and in the kitchen, was uproarious to them. That was the first close look I got of Billy Strayhorn.

Aaron Bridgers: Ben Webster was a strange man. He had a very tender side but also a very rough, tough side. If something made him angry, he could tear a place up and he'd be breaking bar stools if he was drinking. But he was very gentle and almost fatherlike to Strayhorn. And Strayhorn specifically wrote for him. One technical note is that many of Billy Strayhorn's tunes are written in D-flat, which is better suited for wind instruments like Ben's.

Clark Terry (Trumpeter and Bandleader): Unfortunately, Duke had a big problem with Ben Webster. Ben Webster was one of the few people that he fired right on the spot. The guys who were there said they got into this huge beef. And Ben suddenly hauls off and whaps Duke. Ben slapped him, you know? So Duke tells the manager, "Okay. That's it. Pay him off right now and let him go."

—Robert Levi

We talked about civil rights. Strays was very aware of what was going on in the world. The man was politically aware. He wanted to do something for the movement—we both did—and we would talk all night about the situation and the things we thought had to be done. He knew every single person involved in the movement by name. His interest was not casual. The man was as serious as shit.[22]

September 20, 1958, another event changed the direction of the Logans' lives and Strayhorn's too.

Martin Luther King Jr. was at Blumstein's Department Store signing his recent book *Stride Toward Freedom* chronicling the Montgomery bus boycott. A crazed black woman, who believed the NAACP was a front for communism, stepped out of the crowd and stabbed King, nearly killing him. One of the doctors at Harlem Hospital who saved his life was Arthur Logan. In the coming months, the Logans drew King into their social circle. The Logan home became the hub of a salon of artists, intellectuals, musicians, and political figures supportive of King. Marian became one of

Duke Ellington at piano, with dancer Charles "Honi" Coles and Strayhorn looking on, in the Stanley Theatre, circa 1942. Photograph by Charles "Teenie" Harris, American, 1908–1998, Agfa Safety Film, H: 4 in. x W: 5 in., Carnegie Museum of Art, Pittsburgh, Heinz Family Fund.

"LOTUS BLOSSOM" (1945)

Strayhorn's pieces can have multiple and at times enig-matic titles. The first version of "Lotus Blossom" was titled "Hominy," which is a South American food made from treated maize kernels. Why Strayhorn dedicated his attractive composition to this humble ingredient re-mains a mystery. With lyrics by Allen Roy, the song was retitled as "All Roads Lead Back to You." A more fanciful food-based title followed: in 1946, Strayhorn and John-ny Hodges recorded the work as "Charlotte Russe," a classic fruit-based dessert lined with ladyfingers. But the final title, "Lotus Blossom," given in 1959, stuck.

"Lotus Blossom" is one of Strayhorn's most famous waltzes. (He wrote quite a few.) Elegant, beautiful, and seemingly unassuming, the piece is actually quite intricate musically, and not surprisingly, Ellington was

deeply fascinated by it. At the end of the recording session of And His Mother Called Him Bill, Ellington's tribute to his close collaborator of almost thirty years, Ellington sat down at the piano and played "Lotus Blos-som" while the band was packing up. The studio mics hadn't been switched off, and the unplanned perfor-mance was used as the final song on the record. After that, Ellington concluded many of his concerts with Strayhorn's mysterious little waltz.

—Walter van de Leur

RECOMMENDED RECORDING

O Fred Hersch, Passion Flower: Fred Hersch Plays Billy Strayhorn (Nonesuch 1996)

King's close confidants—she was the first northerner to be invited to serve on the board of the Southern Christian Leadership Conference (SCLC) and one of the few women to be in the inner circle of the group. The New York Times (June 2, 1977) referred to her as King's "director of special projects." The Pittsburgh Courier (August 5, 1967) wrote that she was "regarded as being [his] 'right arm.'"

Marian and Arthur bought a single-family brown-stone at 121 West Eighty-Eighth Street in Manhattan late in 1960 and refurbished it. The new plan included a 54-by-20-foot room running the length of the house on the second floor; at its center was an open walnut staircase to the third floor; the ceiling opened to an

awesome two-story view.[23] The stairs became the speaking platform used by King, Rose Kennedy, and countless others to raise money from the Logans' elite guest list. The New York Times reported (Janu-ary 15, 1968): "She does not hesitate to assemble 300 potential donors in her living room." Its grand piano was played by Duke Ellington, Billy Taylor, Luther Hen-derson, and other luminaries. After Dr. King's sermons Billy Strayhorn played the 1941 Joe McCoy/Lil Green "Why Don't You Do Right?" as offertory (the last line of which is "Get out of here and get me some money too") while Marian passed the hat.

Among the Logan circle were Tracy and June Feldman Sugarman. Tracy, at age forty-one, spent

OPPOSITE: The interior of the Logan home at 121 West Eighty-Eighth Street, Manhattan. Martin Luther King Jr. stood on the steps to ad-dress as many as three hundred potential donors while Marian Bruce Logan passed the hat and Billy played "Why Don't You Do Right?"

Donald Lee Hollowell (left, between the lamps), whom *Jet* magazine called "the most brilliant civil rights lawyer practicing in the South" (June 11, 1964), shares his "sacred call" with Logan guests. At the far right (in light suit) is Jack Greenberg, long-time assistant to Thurgood Marshall (1949–1961) and Director-Counsel of the NAACP Legal Defense Fund (1961–1984).

Dignitaries at the Logans' Don Hollowell fund-raiser: Thurgood Marshall (just left of center); Dr. Vaughan Mason, ob-gyn in the U.M.M.G. practice (profile facing Marshall), Aaron Bridgers (center right) with Mercer Ellington. The woman in the foreground (with buckle at her shoulder) is Urban League Guild and NAACP activist Marietta Shivers Dockery, long-time friend of the Logans.

Coretta Scott King, Duke Ellington, and Marian Bruce Logan pose with guest of honor Don Hollowell in the Logan living room.

Bayard Rustin, civil rights leader and chief organizer of the 1963 March on Washington, was a frequent guest of the Logans. The piano was also played by Duke Ellington, Billy Taylor, Luther Henderson, and other luminaries. Billy often played "Lush Life" there.

the Freedom Summer of 1964 in Mississippi preserving images of the voting rights struggle in his illustrations. His work with the Student Nonviolent Coordinating Committee (SNCC) brought him in contact with a more radical element of civil rights leadership than the Logans' guests normally encountered. In his 2007 memoir Sugarman recalled one of the hundreds of nights hosted by Marian and Arthur to raise funds for the cause; Billy's participation was ubiquitous.

One night in the late summer of 1965, shortly after returning from Mississippi, Marian Logan called to ask if we could join them the following Friday evening. In typical Marian style she came straight to the point. "I need your help, Tracy. We've got a

bunch of people who are so uptight with all this talk about 'black power' that we need someone who's been there to explain without bullshit what Stokely Carmichael and Rap Brown are all about. And bring June . . ."

The light from the Logans' brownstone spilled out across Eighty-eighth Street as we approached in the dusk. The large windows facing the street had been opened wide to get the evening breeze after a long, hot August day, and the excited chatter and laughter from the living room were inviting. . . .

The living room was filled with people, only some of whom we had met before. . . . Two horn players from Duke Ellington's band with whom we had shared a birthday party at the Logans' home

Barclay Studios in Paris in the early 1960s, possibly during the recording session for *The Peaceful Side*. Gerhart Lehner, chief engineer at the studio, sits behind Strayhorn.

"KISSING BUG" (1945)

During the final years of the Second World War, Duke Ellington's famous orchestra was getting fewer opportunities to tour due to wartime measures. Without its steady flow of one-nighters, the orchestra landed a number of prolonged broadcast series, such as *Your Saturday Date with the Duke*. Since it was playing more regularly for large radio audiences and often with specific goals, such as the promotion of war bonds, the orchestra had to adjust its repertoire. Strayhorn padded the instrumental and less accessible compositions with an increasing number of vocal arrangements—in most cases, the hit tunes of the day. The orchestra previously had traveled with one female vocalist (the incomparable Ivie Anderson), but in 1945, the band featured no fewer than three women: Kay Davis, Maria Ellington, and Joya Sherrill.

Of these women, Joya Sherrill was arguably the most capable member of the vocal wing. She entered the Ellington organization at the tender age of sixteen and ranks among the few Ellington singers to have actually contributed to the orchestra's repertoire: she is the lyricist of "Kissing Bug." To what was in all likelihood a Rex Stewart riff with Strayhorn chords, Joya added quite decent lyrics that tell the story of a promiscuous lover who's nothing but a kissing bug. One day she'll buy "some bug-a-boo, and that'll put an end to you."

But there is a little surprise. The opening bars of the bridge rhythmically and melodically call up a much more famous song that Strayhorn was to coauthor in the early 1950s: "Satin Doll."

—*Walter van de Leur*

RECOMMENDED RECORDING

⊙ June Christy, *Ballads for Night People* (Capitol 1959)

---

beckoned me to join them at the piano where a dwarf [sic] of a man was quietly evoking echoes of the Duke's endless treasury. . . .

But I could not take my eyes off Jackie Robinson. . . . When Marian approached, I seized her arm with alarm. "Jesus, Marian. You want me to explain black power to Jackie Robinson?"

She grinned wickedly and kissed my cheek. "Yes, Tracila. You know more about it than he does." She moved to the piano and whispered to the pianist, who stopped playing. The room grew silent. "As some of you know, Tracy just got back from the Delta where he's been working with Fannie Lou Hamer. Some of you may have questions he can answer. . . ."

For the next hour I found myself leading a spirited discussion about "black power." . . .

We lingered as the crowd slowly drifted down the stairs and out into the humid summer night, reluctant to leave the Logans. Jackie and Rachel, who had an apartment on the floor above, were unwinding on the couch, and the piano player was softly exploring "Lush Life," seemingly unaware that we were even in the room. Arthur moved to the little bar and brought each of us a nightcap. Jackie Robinson raised his glass and nodded. "To us. All of us."[24]

Hajdu gives the details of the relationship that grew between King and Strayhorn; it became stronger and deeper over time. Others in the Logan circle included A. Philip Randolph and Bayard Rustin, King's gay associate and logistics guru whose greatest accomplishment fulfilled Randolph's long-dreamed March on Washington in August 1963.

1963: Activism in Full Flower

With the opening of the Logans' refurbished salon early in 1963, King's fund-raising parties and gatherings with the New York elite increased. Billy was nearly always there, planning menus, shopping, cooking, and playing piano during the evenings' festivities. He and King stole away to the kitchen for private chats and frequently stayed up until "halfway to dawn," sharing visions for the future.

While Billy's action in the quest for civil equality was often behind the scenes, several events in 1963 put him in the spotlight. Lena Horne had been an intimate friend of Billy's since they met at a Los Angeles production of the 1941 *Jump for Joy* at the Mayan Theater. Due to her insistence from the outset of her career to avoid traditional race casting as a "domestic" or a jungle girl, many old-time black actors thought her presumptuous and a threat to their potential employment. She was accused of trying to "pass."

Her wartime performances for the Tuskegee Airmen (she was "Queen of the 99th"), her appearances in the integrated Hollywood Canteen, her visits to black army bases at her own expense, and her squabbles with the USO over segregated performances (leading to her dismissal from their tours) notwithstanding, she was faulted for not having done enough. During the war, she also aligned herself with progressive groups. Her daughter, Gail Lumet Buckley, wrote of the time:

> Paul Robeson had said, "The artist must speak out"—and Lena had listened. In 1941 she was elected

"Kissing stars," *Metronome* magazine dubbed them. Lena introduced Billy, winner of the *Esquire* Silver Award for Arranging, 1945, to a Los Angeles audience and the nation via radio. He said, "I can't imagine anything more wonderful than receiving this award from the gracious hands of the most favorite of my most favorite people." Lena kissed him; both cried.

> to the board of the Hollywood Independent Citizens Committee for Arts, Sciences and Professions. . . . Lena also made appearances with Assemblyman Augustus Hawkins to promote a Fair Employment Practices Commission in California, and she joined the ranks of Hollywood's activist liberal Democrats, a group that included Bette Davis, Myrna Loy, James Cagney, Joan Blondell, Helen Gahagan and Melvyn Douglas, and Bogart.[25]

She joined the National Council of Negro Women, the Joint Anti-Fascist Refugee Committee, and W. E. B. Du Bois and Paul Robeson's Council on African Affairs, but in October 1947 she committed the

1967

unpardonable—she married Lennie Hayton, a white man. They were wed in Paris—their union was illegal in California—and though the state Supreme Court struck down miscegenation laws in 1948, the Haytons retained their secret until June 1950.

Lena moved more and more into the white entertainment world. On May 24, 1963, Robert Kennedy, Harry Belafonte, and James Baldwin arranged a meeting in New York to discuss what could be done to assuage the anger of young blacks. The gathering included Lena, Lorraine Hansberry (author of *Raisin in the Sun*), psychologist Dr. Kenneth Clark, white actor Rip Torn (a friend of Baldwin's), and a bold young southern black named Jerome Smith. Disabled by the wounds he suffered from white supremacists, Smith convicted Lena with his words. He charged "certainly Mr. Belafonte, Dr. Clark, and Miss Horne—'fortunate Negroes'—who had never seen the inside of a Southern jail, were incapable of understanding it."[26] "After that meeting," Buckley wrote, "Lena called the NAACP and told them that she wanted to go South."[27] They immediately offered her an appearance in Jackson, Mississippi.

Lena craved her brave friend Billy Strayhorn to go with her. She needed him to teach her "Amazing Grace" and "This Little Light of Mine;" she desired his eloquent words for her speech, and wanted his soulful arrangements and beautiful accompaniment. On June 5, 1963, two weeks after the meeting in New York and at their own expense, Lena and Billy departed New York for Jackson. They stopped off in Atlanta where they had an engaging discussion with Julian Bond and made a donation to SNCC.

OPPOSITE: Program cover for the Copasetics' annual dance, 1967. The event was dedicated to the memory of recently departed President Billy Strayhorn who served in that capacity for more than fifteen years.

MARIAN McPARTLAND

PIANIST, BROADCASTER

One of the first songs I played when I started working at the Hickory House in the early '50s was "Lush Life." I learned it from the Nat Cole recording. I hadn't met Billy yet. I just loved the tune—such a beautiful, sad, and sophisticated tune.

There's a feeling in a lot of his music, a sadness, that is so raw and true that it tells you more about Billy than you could learn from meeting him. He was a wonderfully social person and always had a smile for everyone he met. But there was a regretfulness and unhappiness—a sadness inside him that comes across in his music. Just listen to "Lush Life" or "Chelsea Bridge" or "After All" or "Passion Flower" or "Blood Count." He wrote music that was wonderfully upbeat, too—"Take the 'A' Train." But a lot of people could write like that. Nobody else could write "Lush Life," not even Ellington.

I've gotten in a lot of trouble for saying this, but I stand by it, and I'll say it again. Strayhorn's music is all his own, and it stands apart from Ellington's music because it's so deeply abstract and sophisticated.

Billy was the most modest and self-effacing man you could ever meet. I remember him calling for a car to pick him up once. He was on the phone with the dispatcher for the car service, and he said, "Could you possibly accommodate me?" Not "I need a car," [but] "could you possibly accommodate me?" Can you imagine Duke Ellington saying that?

As told to David Hajdu

THE BALLADS AND MORE NEWLY DISCOVERED SONGS

Walter van de Leur: What stands out in the Billy Strayhorn repertoire are his ballads, such as "Something to Live For" and "So This Is Love," which is a piece that surfaced in this new collection that was never known before.

Dianne Reeves (Jazz Vocalist): It's incredible he wrote those songs so long ago; they're songs that I love now, and they feel good, fresh, and new. I mean, God, where were they all these years? Because there were so many great singers who would have just torn them up, like Sarah Vaughan, Ella Fitzgerald, and Carmen McRae; I know they would have loved to have sung these songs.

Chico Hamilton (Drummer and Bandleader): "Something to Live For" really meant something to me. "Swee' Pea" and I used to sing it together. He used to tell me I was the only one who could really sing it. As a matter of fact, my first recording with strings, where I introduced Eric Dolphy, I did "Something to Live For." It's an unbelievable tune, man; it's a gorgeous tune.

Tammy McCann (Jazz Vocalist): Billy Strayhorn wrote his music with the voice in mind. He always had a vision of what he knew that the voice could do, such as the little acrobatics that he wrote for us to do.

Nancy Wilson (Jazz Vocalist): Strayhorn was one of a kind. There will never be anyone else who comes close to his melodic structure. That is the most difficult thing about his music—the melodic structure.

DR: The thing that I love is here are these beautiful lyrics with the harmonies under it that really address what the lyric is saying. Some of the songs that Strayhorn writes are phrased in a way that you have the time to digest what it is that you're singing. You really don't want to move too far away from the way that it's written.

—Robert Levi

The evening of Friday, June 7, more than 2,500 people packed "Negro" Masonic Temple on Lynch Street in Jackson. Lena sang a medley of freedom songs arranged by Billy and echoed the words he wrote for her. She said, "The battle . . . being fought here in Jackson, as elsewhere in the South, is our nation's primary crisis. Let it be understood that the courage and grim determination of the Negro people in these cities of the South have challenged the moral integrity of the entire nation."[28]

From the front row, Byron De La Beckwith and two of his cronies blew cigarette smoke at Lena and Billy while they performed.[29] When asked to extinguish their smokes, the three stormed away. Beckwith shot and killed Medgar Evers four days later just after midnight, Wednesday, June 12.

Evers's death led the national news that morning; coincidentally, Horne was scheduled to appear on *The Today Show.* It was not until arriving at the studio, sitting in the holding room watching a girl showing self-defense exercises on the monitor, that she heard of Evers's killing.

I don't really remember what I said on that show, except that the girl who had been demonstrating judo reminded me of a class I had attended

OPPOSITE, FROM TOP: On November 14, 1965, Ellington was honored with an Urban League Guild Special Salute. Lena sang "I've Got It Bad and That Ain't Good," to Billy's accompaniment. § Marian and Arthur Logan joined Lena, Billy and two thousand other guests to honor Ellington at the Rainbow Room of the Rockefeller Plaza, November 14, 1965.

"BILLY STRAYHORN WAS MY RIGHT ARM, MY LEFT ARM, ALL THE EYES IN THE BACK OF MY HEAD, MY BRAINWAVES IN HIS HEAD, AND HIS IN MINE."

—DUKE ELLINGTON

Duke Ellington, Willie "The Lion" Smith, George Wein, and Billy Strayhorn, back turned, with two other men standing in the wings of stage for jazz workshop, Pittsburgh Jazz Festival, in Civic Arena, June 18–20, 1965. *Photograph by Charles "Teenie" Harris, American, 1908–1998, Kodak Safety Film, H: 4 in. x W: 5 in., Carnegie Museum of Art, Pittsburgh, Heinz Family Fund.*

in Jackson in which they had been teaching little nine- to twelve-year-olds self protection, how to protect their bodies, how to cover their heads if they were knocked down and someone started to kick them.

Medgar's death had so filled me with horror that all I could see were miles and miles of little Negro children lying in the knee-chest position, protecting themselves from white people. I talked about that. And I talked about the terrible loneliness of the Negro child when his mother first explains to

him what it is to be a "Nigger" and he knows that he is, from that day forward, forever set apart.[30]

The matter of bail money for jailed activists was on the minds of the Logans and their friends Jackie and Rachel Robinson. After King and Ralph David Abernathy's solitary confinement in Birmingham from Good Friday (April 12) to April 20, supporters of the demonstrators knew the importance of a fund that quickly supplied bail money for arrested activists. The Robinsons offered the grounds of their

"PORTRAIT OF A SILK THREAD" (1945)

After Billy Strayhorn passed away, Gregory Morris, his nephew and executor of the estate, cleared out his uncle's apartment in New York. He carefully packed the reams of handwritten music in bankers' boxes and stored them for future use. In the decades that followed, no one seemed particularly interested in Strayhorn, who remained a footnote in the glorious career of Duke Ellington. In the 1990s, a new generation of jazz scholars started to delve into the numerous manuscript collections that became available and ask critical questions.

Strayhorn's personal papers helped these scholars thoroughly reassess his collaboration with Ellington, grasp the extent of his impressive contributions to the orchestra's repertoire, and better understand his musical fingerprints and individual style. As a bonus, dozens of never-performed masterpieces turned up in the forms of compositions written for various orchestras and occasions, music for shows, music for the theater,

arrangements for Pittsburgh territory bands, unknown songs, classical piano works, and many more.

Among these unknown works was "Portrait of a Silk Thread," a piece of stunning beauty. Its title gives few clues to the work's background or meaning, yet, as is the rule with virtually all of Strayhorn's compositions, the answer lies in the music rather than in its title. "Portrait of a Silk Thread" is about sound, harmony and dissonance, and form and structure, but above all, it's about deep musical expression.

—Walter van de Leur

RECOMMENDED RECORDING

⦿ Dutch Jazz Orchestra, *Portrait of a Silk Thread: Newly Discovered Works of Billy Strayhorn* (Challenge 1995)

---

estate in Stamford, Connecticut, for an "Afternoon of Jazz" on June 30. Strayhorn was one of the artists to perform on behalf of the cause on a sweltering day for a crowd of six hundred. Dave Brubeck, Dizzy Gillespie, Cannonball Adderley, Joya Sherrill, Jimmy Rushing, and James Moody also joined the event that raised $15,000 for the SCLC. *Ebony* (October 1963) chronicled the summer in which nearly a quarter of a million dollars was raised for SCLC, NAACP, CORE, and SNCC by "those celebrities whose names have long graced night club, theater and concert hall marquees."

Ellington is not listed in that *Ebony* article. He continued his on-the-road and in-the-air testimony; his travelogue records he was in Europe from January 9 until March 15, then doing domestic concerts and

Duke Ellington, Billy Strayhorn, and copyist Thomas Whaley at a recording session in New York for Ellington's *My People*. This production was directed by Billy at Chicago's McCormick Place in 1963 in honor of the hundredth anniversary of the Emancipation Proclamation.

On October 5, 1963, Billy arrived in Madras, India, on the State Department tour. Ellington was left in the hospital in New Delhi on September 28. Billy led the orchestra until Duke was able to rejoin the group in Rang Bhavan on October 8.

recording until May 25. He flew again to Europe where he worked until June 25. He appeared on *The Tonight Show* July 4, at the Newport Jazz Festival (July 5–6), and at the Ravinia Festival (July 10–12); recorded in New York (July 18); and appeared at Basin Street East in a series of dates (July 19, 26, August 2, 3, and 9). Additional one-nighters filled the empty evenings. Yet there was more: the major tasks of midsummer revolved around preparations of music for the Stratford (Ontario) Shakespeare Festival (July) and for a new work for Chicago titled *My People*.[31]

The Chicago celebration of the centennial of Lincoln's Emancipation Proclamation included an exhibit titled "Century of Negro Progress." It was held at McCormick Place and was supported by twenty-one major US corporations. Ellington was invited to write a musical production to run August 16 to September 2 at the 5,000-seat Arie Crown Theater, one of the largest seating capacities in the city. "A pageantlike revue about black history,"[32] copyist Thomas Whaley described the concept:

> He had the people coming up from the pit, they were in rags, my people, our people in rags coming up and then at the end they were doctors and lawyers and everything. And he developed it and oh, it was beautiful and the last thing was "What is Colour, What is Virtue?"[33]

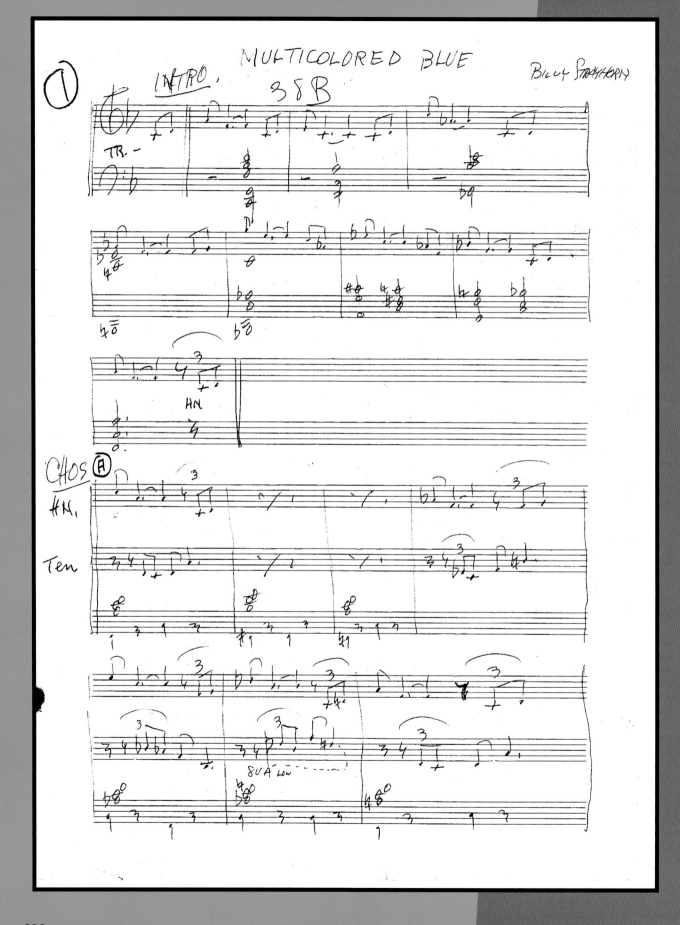

Duke "felt he was making a racial contribution," said singer Joya Sherrill.[34] Ellington described the chaotic birthing:

I was writing the music for this show and for the Stratford Shakespearean Festival, Stratford, Ontario production of *Timon of Athens* at the same time. This meant going to Stratford to work, flying into Chicago to rehearse the choirs of Irving Bunton and Charles Moore, doing my one-nighters with the band in between, dashing back to New York to work with the choreographers Alvin Ailey and Tally Beatty, returning to Stratford, and so on and on. . . . I wrote the music, words, and orchestrations for *My People*, directed it, and did everything but watch the loot.[35]

Ellington fully intended to continue his road work throughout the run of the show so Strayhorn was deputized to "personally supervise" the orchestra made up of nine Ellington veterans and fill-ins, play piano, and accompany the band on the road when Ellington's presence was required in Chicago. As always, Strayhorn's role was much broader than acknowledged. The original cast album merely credits him with celeste. Jimmy Jones clarified:

Strayhorn did some writing, we did some things out of *Paris Blues* and *Black, Brown and Beige*—he just went in the book, and then Duke, the old man, wrote some more things.[36]

One of the new pieces ended up being a dramatic highlight in the show. "King Fit the Battle of Alabam" featured a lyric and melody written by Ellington and first sung by him at the Newport Festival in July. The setting for the Irving Bunton Singers stopped the show.

Singer Jimmy McPhail described Strayhorn's motivation for his work in *My People*. He said, "Billy

MULTI-COLORED BLUE (1945/1950)

As a child, Strayhorn spent summers with his grandparents in Hillsborough, North Carolina—a welcome alternative to the often tense domestic situation at home in Pittsburgh. In Hillsborough, he learned to play the piano, and his grandmother instilled in him a lifelong love for flowers, which he expressed in many pieces. "Multi-Colored Blue" is one of them.

The history of the piece is somewhat complex. It started in 1945 as an instrumental called "Violet Blue," which is the part that opens the tune. In the 1950s, he expanded the song with lyrics and added another melody. This he retitled as "Multi-Colored Blue." In the lyrics, Strayhorn contrasts the different colors of flowers with a blue heart.

—*Walter van de Leur*

RECOMMENDED RECORDING

◉ Billy Strayhorn Sextet, *Lush Life* (1965; Red Barron 1992)

was happy to do it because it was a good thing to do, a statement against racism."[37] Strayhorn had even greater statements to make. He took days off during the run, left Chicago, and returned to New York. The occasion was the annual benefit dance of the Copasetics, a social and service group composed primarily of dancers, who tapped Billy as their president shortly after the group formed in 1950. He wrote words and music annually for their hot ticket dance for the Harlem elite. The traditional time for the gala was the last Monday of September. Because of the Ellington orchestra's upcoming fourteen-week State Department tour to the Middle East, Billy would be required to leave the

Eddie West, a member of the vaudeville dance trio Chocolatiers, was a charter member of the Copasetics. His painting of the fraternity depicts President Strayhorn at the end of the piano, holding a music score. The painting is now in the collection of Jane Goldberg, tap dancer, journalist, and historian.

country September 6. The Copasetics bumped up their show from September 30 to August 26.[38]

Typically, the Copasetics shows were lighthearted romps based on a familiar theme that could serve as a foil for the talents and antics of the group. In 1961 it was *On the Riviera*, a send-up of the 1951 Danny Kaye film; in 1962 it was *Anchors Aweigh*, a parody of the 1945 Frank Sinatra and Gene Kelly farce. But this one—in 1963—was Billy's parallel to Duke's *My People*. It

was a laugh-to-keep-from-crying topical piece titled *Down Dere*. Hajdu described it as "a joyful ride on the 'freedom train' of civil rights."[39] Marshall and Jean Stearns added: "That year, in line with explosive political developments, they decided to draw upon the tradition of acrobatic dance."[40]

An eyewitness account, probably by Cholly Atkins and Honi Coles, delivers details about Billy's parallel to Duke's *My People*:

A dozen little old men hobble on stage dressed as hayseeds with gray beards, each with one hand on his aching back, the other hand tapping with a cane, as if he were blind. In quavering tones they sing "Down Dere," promising that there'll be some changes made in the South. Suddenly the band takes off on "Jumpin' at the Woodside"—one of Count Basie's flag-wavers—and the little old men explode into acrobatic anarchy. It is organized; that is, they are all doing the same things simultaneously, but the steps are wild, the effect frantic.

To top it off, Deighton Boyce catapults on stage dressed as a sweet old lady and throws himself into rows of cartwheels, flips, and spins, with wig, shawl, and skirts flying. He is tumbling in the traditional acrobatic manner, but it is all precisely on the beat. A semblance of order is restored as the dancers exit on an imaginary bus to the tune of "Alabamy Bound."

Other acts come and go. The featured speaker is Dick Gregory. . . . For the finale the old men are back in flannel shirts and overalls with an energetic challenge dance—each soloing in turn.

Once more Boyce shoots out from the wings with a front no-hands somersault over five dancers lined up on the floor and then, with a running start, slides the length of the stage on his stomach and off into the orchestra pit with a loud crash. The scramble of the musicians to get out of the way is genuine.[41]

"SNIBOR" (1947)

On October 17, 1947, Claude Thornhill and his orchestra recorded a new piece by Illinois Jacquet and Sir Charles Thompson named "Robbins Nest." The piece was a salute to a popular radio show of the day by the same title, hosted by Fred Robbins. Unfortunately for Strayhorn, he had just written a piece dedicated to the same show and had titled it accordingly. The solution to the title problem was Strayhornesque: he spelled the first half of the title backward and dropped a letter in the process—his "Robbins Nest" became "Snibor."

It is interesting to note that Strayhorn's "Snibor" was composed along the lines of an earlier, at the time unrecorded, work: "Matinee." Though more unconventional in its structure, "Matinee" shares a number of concepts with "Snibor," such as the subdued tutti instrumentation of the first chorus, the key of D-flat (Strayhorn's favorite), and a number of offbeat phrases. "Snibor" has another relative: "A Midnight in Paris," composed and recorded almost fifteen years later. "A Midnight in Paris" is in the same key as its '40s siblings, and it is built on a theme that strongly resembles "Snibor."

"Snibor" premiered at Carnegie Hall in December 1947 as "The New Look." That title was possibly a nod to Christian Dior's 1947 fashion line, greeted by the editor in chief of *Harper's Bazaar* as "such a new look!" Not long after the concert, the orchestra waxed the piece in the recording studio. But "Snibor" possibly became best known through its inclusion in that timeless tribute Ellington paid to his collaborator on the album *And His Mother Called Him Bill*.

—*Walter van de Leur*

RECOMMENDED RECORDING

○ Michael Hashim, *MultiColoured Blue* (Hep 1999)

As always, Billy's Copasetics show was a sellout. Strayhorn's title song, "Down Dere," bears interesting lyrical comparison to Ellington's "King Fit the Battle of Alabam." Written the same summer, they demonstrate the mood of the time and the two crusaders.

Strayhorn's "Shame of It—Down Dere"

Oh the shame of it—the shame of it
Calling it democracy but living in hypocrisy
The shame of it down dere
We've fought our battle all these years
Grown old and still ain't free
So raise your voices loud and clear
Cause a change has got to be
Down dere
Down dere, big things a coming
Down dere things ain't the same
Down dere youngsters hummin'
Waiting for the Freedom train
Down dere no pickin' cotton
Down dere just picketing
Down dere Tommins forgotten
Waiting for the Freedom train
Train is comin' had to be,
Train is comin' to set us Free
Train is comin', comin' fast,
Train is comin' down dere at last
Down dere bail is an honor
Down dere nothing in vain
Down dere Ol' Bull Conner
Scared of the Freedom train. [42]

Ellington's "King Fit the Battle of Alabam"

King fit the battle of Alabam,
Birmingham, Ala-ba-bam,
King fit the battle of Alabam,
And the Bull got nasty—ghastly—nasty
Bull turned the hoses on the church people
And the water came splashing—dashing—crashing
Freedom rider—ride
Freedom rider—go to town
Y'all and us—gonna get on the bus
Y'all aboard—sit down, sit tight, you're right . . .
Little babies fit the battle of police dogs—mongrel
  police
And the dogs came growling—howling—growling
And when the dog saw the baby wasn't afraid
He turned to his Uncle Bull and said
The baby acts like he don't give a damn
Are you sure we're still in Alabam? [43]

After *Down Dere*, Strayhorn immediately headed to Washington, D.C., where he joined A. Philip Randolph and Bayard Rustin in final preparations for the storied March on Washington. Randolph accepted Billy's offer to provide people-power to the historic event. Billy "loaned out" his sixteen-year-old niece Alyce Claerbaut for her typing skills; she worked for Randolph in the run-up to the event at the March office in Harlem.[44]

The Willard Hotel in D.C. was the site of a block of rooms occupied by King, the Logans, Billy, and others in the inner circle. Reunited with his great friend Martin, Strayhorn "talked off his ear about Ellington's show and how wonderful it was. Martin promised to go see it, and after that, he did. Arthur and I took him, and

OPPOSITE: "'He's great.' 'She's great.' That was the thing he said more than anything. It was part of his philosophy, his approach to being alive, which was very generous, very open, almost too much so." *Bill Patterson, psychologist and member of Billy and Aaron's* **New York circle of friends.**

Musicians Charles Bell, Billy Strayhorn, Duke Ellington, Mary Lou Williams, Dizzy Gillespie, Earl "Fatha" Hines, Billy Taylor, and Willie "The Lion" Smith, on stage for a jazz workshop at the Pittsburgh Jazz Festival in the Civic Arena, June 18–20, 1965. *Photograph by Charles "Teenie" Harris, American, 1908–1998, Kodak Safety Film, H: 4 in. x W: 5 in., Carnegie Museum of Art, Pittsburgh, Heinz Family Fund.*

Six women, including Ethel Waters seated third from left, and four men, including Billy Strayhorn seated on left, some holding paper cups, gathered around end table with birthday cake, in Stanley Theatre with leaf patterned sofa and carpet, and steamer trunk on left, circa 1944. *Photograph by Charles "Teenie" Harris, American, Agfa Superpan Press Safety Film, 1908–1998, H: 4 in. x W: 5 in., Carnegie Museum of Art, Pittsburgh, Heinz Family Fund.*

LENA HORNE

SINGER, ACTOR, ACTIVIST

It's very hard for me to talk about him. He became my brother but more than a brother. I fell in love with him.

It was very natural for us to be friends. If we couldn't see each other, we talked every day on the phone. This was the only relationship of this type I've ever had. He decoded me. I didn't have to make statements to him. He sensed what I wanted to do or what I wanted to say. He understood me like no one understood me. He knew me better than I knew myself. He studied me. He watched me comb my hair and watched what I wore.

If I was low, he'd sit in the room with me, and we'd talk. Maybe we wouldn't even talk. We'd just sit together.

He recognized the strength in people, and he saw their weaknesses, and he accepted them. He was a humanist. He was always trying to get me to loosen up and be more accepting. He understood people's frailties. He was frail himself. He knew that I was frail, too, but I disguised it by acting tough. He really wanted me to open myself up and face that life was sometimes bitchy, sometimes hard, and sometimes quite beautiful.

Everybody knew that he was a fantastic musician. There was a great passionate sensuality to his music. The things that he wrote were very, very strong—but also sensitive, almost feminine. His music was sensuous, passionate beyond romance. The things he wrote were even about trees and flowers and beauty. I never knew a man like that.

Not enough gratitude was paid to him. Duke was monumental in his acceptance by the world, but he also had a monumental ego. Many artists are like that, and it must have been hard for him to understand how music so magnificent could come out of this humble little man Billy.

We were close-close. We talked about life, and we talked about death. When he grew sick, he had—I don't know what to call it. It was a kind of bravery but not exactly bravery. It was just an attitude, a calmness. The death he saw coming ahead for him was another phase, and he was looking at it and studying it like he would examine a piece of music.

He was like, actually, a physical part of me. He's inside me to this day, and I dream of him. For many years after he left, whenever I was nervous about a piece that I thought I'd do or a project I had to start on, he'd always come in a dream and be very soothing about it, and I'd know it would be all right.

As told to David Hajdu

---

that was where he met Edward for the first time."[45] Upon meeting, Ellington suggested to King that they go to a rehearsal Billy was conducting. Once there he asked the company to present "King Fit the Battle of Alabam" to the man it honored. Marian Bruce Logan recalled that King was "very impressed, very proud. It was quite a moment." Ellington later gave the original manuscript to King.

After *My People* closed September 2, Billy, Duke, and the orchestra prepared to leave for the State Department tour. They departed September 6 from Idlewild Airport. On September 26, Ellington was left in the hospital at New Delhi; Billy played piano and directed the band until Duke rejoined them October 8. They were in Ankara, Turkey, when word came that Kennedy had been assassinated. The remainder of the tour was cancelled, and they arrived back in New York November 29.

Early in 1964, Dr. Logan diagnosed Billy's cancer. He was still able to work for most of the next two years, but fatigue kept him from frequent travel and from the pace of activism that had characterized the apex of activity in 1963. His conversations with King became deeper when Martin's schedule brought him to New York. When King received the Nobel Peace Prize, the Logans joined him on the trip to Stockholm to accept. In the second week of December 1964, Billy went with them to (now) Kennedy Airport to see his friends fly away, encouraging them all with shouts of "Bravo!"[46]

BILLY STRAYHORN'S SEXUALITY

Was Billy Strayhorn a frightened little gay man? Willing to deny or remain acquiescently silent about his genius in order to pursue private relationships with his lovers?

Strayhorn was oppressed because of his sexual orientation, just as he was for his racial identity. Yet he was resilient. He became a remarkably successful musician—not at all obscure, though the persons with whom and systems in which he operated rarely credited him fully for his brilliant work. An old acquaintance said that three out of any four people who knew Strayhorn would have described him as their best friend.[47] He had some very psychologically healthy romantic relationships—along with some tragically failed ones.

He knew he was gay from his first sexual awakening: in his early teens, while walking with his friend

"ORSON" (1950)

Strayhorn met actor and director Orson Welles on the West Coast in the 1940s. At the time, there were rumors about an Ellington-Strayhorn-Welles collaboration, but it did not take place until later when Welles asked Ellington to write music for a play set to premiere in Paris, titled *Le Temps Court*. It was a reworking of *Faust* in a program under the heading *The Blessed and the Damned*. Ellington gracefully declined but suggested Strayhorn take on the assignment. Strayhorn traveled to Paris to prepare the score on-site. The production was ill-fated, and nothing came of the music, which was written for a six-piece ensemble. One of the pieces was dedicated to the play's female protagonist, Helen of Troy, titled "Helen's Theme." Strayhorn later adapted it for his band and retitled it "Orson," a work that is too little known. The Ellington orchestra recorded the piece only once in a strangely abridged version that didn't do justice to the composer's intentions. The complete score has much to offer: Strayhorn crafted an intricate orchestral setting around one of his most inspired and emotionally charged themes.

—Walter van de Leur

RECOMMENDED RECORDING

◉ Dutch Jazz Orchestra, *So This Is Love: More Newly Discovered Works of Billy Strayhorn* (Challenge 2002)

Harry Herforth in Frick Park, they talked "mostly about books and music. I know we did not talk about girls. There was no sexual reference at all. We didn't talk about race relationships. We just seemed to accept he was black; I was white. So what?"[48] Herforth was straight; Billy was gay. So what?

"Lately, personnel changes have prompted the comment that what I call the Ellington Effect has been replaced by something different. . . . The same comment accompanied my arrival, but . . . I think my playing and writing style is totally different from Ellington's. *Billy Strayhorn, 1952, as told to Nat Shapiro and Nat Hentoff in* Hear Me Talkin' to Ya.

One of Billy's two copyrighted pieces with songwriting partner Raymond Wood. The opening line may reflect a deeper involvement between the two men.

"ALL DAY LONG" (1951)

One of Strayhorn's favorite techniques was the use of metric shifts, or so-called hemioles, in his compositions. The most common form of a hemiole is the division of an orchestral figure into three-beat segments while the underlying meter is 4/4, which tremendously adds to the rhythmic drive of a piece. Strayhorn's work is full of such hemioles, from the saxophone ensemble in "Rain Check" to the modulatory section at the end of the second chorus of his famous "Take the 'A' Train." With its rhythmically displaced intro and off-center theme, the cryptically titled "All Day Long" is a showcase of such polymetric writing.

In his liner notes to *The Complete Capitol Recordings,* jazz writer Stanley Dance was not very favorable toward "All Day Long." Stating that it "was all section and ensemble work," he added that he heard "uncompleted experimenting in orchestral textures" in the piece. Yet, when considering Strayhorn's oeuvre, the work is rather conservative and not too experimental at all. After his creative outburst in the first half of the 1940s, Strayhorn seems to have invested somewhat less in innovation in the early 1950s.

While not as visionary as the later "U.M.M.G." or as deeply moving as some of his great ballads that lay ahead ("Pretty Girl," "Isfahan"), "All Day Long" is genuine Strayhornia, a highly rewarding and hard-swinging piece, and a tour de force for the entire orchestra. The piece sports some of Strayhorn's most tightly designed ensembles and a number of remarkably dense, yet transparent, full-band contrapuntal passages.

—Walter van de Leur

RECOMMENDED RECORDING

○ Duke Ellington and His Orchestra, *And His Mother Called Him Bill* (Columbia 1967)

In 1934 Billy experienced what was likely his first sexual liaison, with Raymond Wood. Hajdu hints at their involvement in *Lush Life*[49] and proclaims it more confidently in Robert Levi's 2007 film. In October 1934, Wood and Strayhorn copyrighted two songs, the lyrics of which are inferior to anything else that came from Strayhorn's pen. They must be Raymond's. The lyric of the first, "You Lovely Little Devil," reflects some conversation the writers had about Shakespeare, a literary influence we know was strong in Billy's mind. The critical line is "Oh won't you be my Julie and I'll be your Romeo."

The second lyric leaves little ambiguity about the contrasting identity of these lovers:

Queer how we first met
We loved each other so
How can you say we're through
Can't it be as before?

Chorus
I begged you not to go
You know I loved you so
Dear, I'm still begging you

You begged me for my heart
Then tore it all apart
Dear, I'm still begging you.

The night that we first met
We started right in to pet
And now there's nothing left
But sorrow and regret
It's you I'm thinking of
You are the one I love
Dear, I'm still begging you. [50]

Equally telling is the pair of compositions in the Billy Strayhorn collection of manuscripts that Van de

Pearl Allen Wood with four of her children: Raymond is on the right, leaning in. Billy met Ray Wood shortly after completing high school. They formed an artistic partnership, and Wood cowrote Billy's first two copyrighted works: "I'm Still Beggin' You" and "You Lovely Little Devil." Wood, and Billy's relationship with him, likely inspired a number of early "lost love" works: "Something to Live For," "Your Love Has Faded," and perhaps even "Lush Life."

Leur dates earlier—from winter 1934. The first valse, inscribed with Billy's signature, reflects his excellent classical training and sensibilities; the second, with a composer attribution in block letters "Raymond Wood," the musical notation still in Billy's hand, is inferior in quality. The second might be the composition of Wood harmonized or transcribed by Billy from the other's dictation.[51] An exchange of musical valentines (as it were), by the young innocents is not far-fetched. Was "Life Is Lonely"—the first title for "Lush Life"—the lament of their parting? "Life is awful again, and *only*

ROSEMARY CLOONEY

SINGER

We were recording the *Blue Rose* album, me with the Duke Ellington Orchestra, and he came out to California to work with me. The record was entirely his idea. He wanted me to sing with Ellington orchestra, and he oversaw the whole recording.

I couldn't travel, because I was pregnant and having trouble with the pregnancy. I was really suffering with morning sickness, and he was like a best friend with me. He would come up to my room and sit on the bed, and I'd say, "Oh, God, I'm going to throw up again." And he'd say, "Now, you've got to keep something on your stomach." And so he would bring me crackers and milk, and he would say, "Don't get up—don't move until you just have the crackers and milk." He baked me an apple pie. He really did—he baked me a pie. And he'd sit there. He was just like my best friend. He really, truly was. He cared about the baby. He watched out for me.

He was brilliant as a vocal coach, of course. I remember [when] we were working on "I'm Checkin' Out, Goombye." He said, "This shouldn't be angry. It should be, 'I've got you now, you rascal.'" It wasn't the end of the world for the singer of the song. It was "I've caught up with you now, and I'm out of here."

He said, "Don't be angry. Make your own way," and it was almost like he was giving me his whole philosophy.

As told to David Hajdu

Ellington and his extended entourage help Billy celebrate his birthday in elegant surroundings.

Billy enjoys a night out with partner Aaron Bridgers and friend Billie Holiday at Barney Josephson's Café Society Uptown, "the wrong place for the Right people." The club opened in 1940 on East Fifty-Eighth Street, between Lexington and Park Avenues, and like its older sibling Downtown, it was one of the first places where "blacks and whites worked together behind the footlights and sat together out front."

last year everything seemed so sure." Do other lyrics written about this time also reflect first unsuccessful attempts at love? "Let Nature Take Its Course," "Your Love Has Faded," "Something to Live For"?

In 1936 when he was twenty-one, Billy sang "Lush Life" for Harry Herforth. The word "gay" stares at us from the first line of the lyric. Did Billy know the coded use of the word that had already begun among the sophisticated composers in New York? Sure. He

subscribed to the *New Yorker* in high school and clearly knew the linguistic style of Cole Porter and Noël Coward. Herforth heard Billy's lyric in just that manner. Strayhorn, he said, "admitted a marvelous and undying admiration for the lyrics of Cole Porter, those super-sophisticated things. That's where he got his model, if he needed one. But 'Lush Life' is as super-sophisticated as anything Porter came up with."[52] It is no more difficult to grasp that he knew

I USED TO VISIT ALL
THE VERY GAY PLACES
/ THOSE COME
WHAT MAY PLACES /
WHERE ONE RELAXES
ON THE AXIS / OF
THE WHEEL OF LIFE /
TO GET THE FEEL OF
LIFE / FROM JAZZ
AND COCKTAILS

—"LUSH LIFE"

"BOO-DAH" (1953)

One of Strayhorn's most appropriate nicknames was Buddha for his tendency to quietly sit and savor the company of his friends. He must have liked it better than Swee' Pea or Weely—names the Ellingtonians used for him—because he dedicated an entire composition to this sobriquet. The smart title of the tune "Boo-Dah" mimics the phrasing of the music, like some of the works of the boppers: Strayhorn has the brass say "boo-dah" throughout the song, and, as with some of his other compositions ("After All," "Lately"), the title fits the first notes of the theme as well—a sure sign of Strayhorn's quest for the "marriage of music and words," as his collaborator-friend once called it.

The first, and rather little-known, recording of the work was made in April 1953 at a time when the Ellington orchestra was struggling to survive in a world that had largely turned its back on big bands. It was also the time when the partnership between Strayhorn and Ellington was seriously cooling off, mainly because Strayhorn was unhappy with the lack of recognition he received for his work.

Strayhorn did not live to hear the orchestra record a glorious second version of "Boo-Dah," some fourteen years later. The Ellingtonians cut this version as the opener for the highly praised tribute album *And His Mother Called Him Bill* a month after Strayhorn passed away at the age of fifty-one.

—*Walter van de Leur*

RECOMMENDED RECORDING

◉ Duke Ellington and His Orchestra, *And His Mother Called Him Bill* (Columbia 1967)

---

this specific use of the word than that he described with such accuracy the lure of the drink or the "ease the bite of it" that Paris could and later did provide for him.

There is no doubt about the relationship of Strayhorn with Aaron Bridgers once he arrived in New York. They too were musically simpatico, and they moved to declare their love by living together and entertaining Billy's new colleagues from the Ellington orchestra as a couple in their apartment "straight out of the pages of *Esquire* magazine."[53] Billy met Haywood Williams through Aaron. Bridgers met Williams at a party and got him a job as a bellman in the Kenmore Hall Hotel on Lexington Avenue where Aaron worked as an elevator operator. It was Williams who helped connect Aaron and Billy with his landlord so they might rent another of his properties—315 Convent Avenue.[54]

Billy and Aaron lived together until Bridgers left for Paris in 1947. They remained intimate. Whenever Billy visited Paris (as he did several times after 1950), they found their relationship had changed little. Even after they were physically separated for eighteen years, it was Aaron to whom Billy turned when his cancer became critical. Writing to Bridgers on July 27, 1965, Billy confided about his upcoming surgery, asking Aaron to keep the news private, as he had discussed it with no one else. He signed the letter:

LUV B.S.
XXXX XXXX AD INFINITUM[55]

Aaron Bridgers was the love of Billy's life. They met within months of Billy's arrival in New York, lived together in the 1940s, and were reunited during Strayhorn's many trips to Paris after 1950. After Billy's death, Bridgers flew to New York and mourned alongside Billy's other partners, friends, and relatives.

BILLY STRAYHORN AND POST-BOP MODERNISM

Billy Strayhorn displayed a versatility that was uncharacteristic of other famous jazz composers. Strayhorn's music was always innovative and never went out of style.

Fred Hersch: Some of Strayhorn's music, I find a bit Thelonious Monk-like; I also find him connected to the first generation of post-bop jazz composers, like Tadd Dameron. Strayhorn's career really bridged a large swath of the development of jazz: bebop, big band, and into the cool period.

David Baker: Billy Strayhorn was able to intuit the way music was moving. Dizzy Gillespie and Charlie Parker—major figures of the next important generation in jazz—were very interested in what Strayhorn was doing that was in no way a holdover from the swing era.

Dianne Reeves: Strayhorn left Ellington in the mid-1950s, and when I heard his song, "The Flowers Die of Love," I thought, "Wow, that's really a departure. It sounds timeless and has a very contemporary quality; it's very beautiful."

"The Flowers Die of Love" is a very hypnotic song that is trancelike, about someone fixated on something they can't have; it makes me feel that sometimes you can love something to death; this was a poem that was attractive to him.

—Robert Levi

After Aaron's departure for Paris on New Year's in 1948, Strayhorn did not live openly with another lover until 1958 when Francis Goldberg moved into Billy's apartment at 15 West 106th Street. He met "Goldie" and his twin brother, Frank, in Los Angeles in October 1942, and after the war, he welcomed them into the Aaron/Billy circle of gay men in New York. Billy and Goldie's relationship might have been a sexual one throughout this period, but they became identifiable spouses ten years after Bridgers moved to Paris.

In 1950, Charles "Cookie" Cook, another member of Billy's intimate group of gay men, brought Strayhorn to what was to be one of the most significant circles of influence in his life. It was he who suggested to LeRoy Myers, James "Chuckles" Walker, and Luther "Slim" Preston that they invite Billy to join Copasetics, the group they were forming to honor Bojangles Robinson. Billy brought Francis and Frank Goldberg along; Francis later became treasurer.[56]

Cholly Atkins, another founding member, stated a significant insight into the feeling the Copasetics had about Billy's sexuality.

Billy met Francis "Goldie" Goldberg and his twin brother, Frank, in Los Angeles in 1942. After the war the Goldbergs became part of the circle of gay friends that gathered in Billy's New York home. Billy and Goldie became lovers and lived together in the late 1950s.

Billy in a publicity photograph with a non-sequitur doe. In Billy's era everyone smoked—everyone, especially jazz musicians. The smoky jazz photo was as ubiquitous as the music and the habit.

In 1954, Luther Henderson and Billy Strayhorn attempted to escape their frustrations with Ellington's co-opting of their work by collaborating on a Broadway show, *Rose-Colored Glasses*. Duke put the kibosh on their musical partnership, but Henderson and Strayhorn retained their deep friendship. In September 1956 Billy was best man for the wedding of Henderson and Stephanie Le Beau Locke. "Stevie" died only four days after Billy in 1967—also a victim of cancer.

On an outing with Luther Henderson and Stephanie Le Beau Henderson, circa 1956.

DON PERLIMPLÍN: "LOVE, LOVE," "THE FLOWERS DIE OF LOVE," "SPRITE MUSIC," "WOUNDED LOVE" (1953)

Along with his more visible work for Ellington, Strayhorn was involved with other orchestras and productions as well. In 1953, he wrote music for an off-Broadway production by the Artists Theatre. The company staged a surrealist play by the Spanish author Federico García Lorca (1898–1936) called *The Love of Don Perlimplín and Belisa in the Garden*. This version celebrated both black and gay pride—a radical approach largely conceptualized by Strayhorn. Four of his compositions have survived: one instrumental work, "Sprite Music," and three songs based on poems in the play: "Wounded Love," "The Flowers Die of Love," and "Love, Love."

Departing from his many harmonically and rhythmically intricate scores, Strayhorn here used simplicity as an expressive tool. In the majestic and at times almost Schubert-ian "The Flowers Die of Love," he designed a simple melody over a repeated piano figure. In "Love, Love"—in reference to García Lorca's use of water as a metaphor for erotic passion—Strayhorn's music is full of aquatic metaphors, from the waltz-time, which quietly flows underneath, to the rapid, cascading vocal runs. Throughout, his piano accompaniment is strongly suggestive of the piano works of the French composer Francis Poulenc, whose spirit is felt in "Sprite Music."

"Wounded Love," set to the most famous passage in García Lorca's play, conveys a tremendous emotional depth. All of Don Perlimplín's conflicting emotions are expressed in the dramatic descending gesture that opens the song. Strayhorn used this figure as a love motif to underscore the key recurrences of "love." He also designed a death motif in the vocal part, a note pattern first heard in "dying of love" that recurs in "bleeding heart." At each occurrence of the singer's death motif, Strayhorn's piano accompaniment provides the love motif, thus musically securing the connection between the two. In the meantime, this connection articulates one of the main subtexts of García Lorca's poem (love and death are related) and sums up the central theme of the play.

—Walter van de Leur

> Departing from his many harmonically and rhythmically intricate scores, Strayhorn here used simplicity as an expressive tool.

RECOMMENDED RECORDINGS

◉ Dutch Jazz Orchestra, *Something to Live For: The Music of Billy Strayhorn* (Challenge 2002)

◉ Dianne Reeves, *Lush Life* (Blue Note 2007)

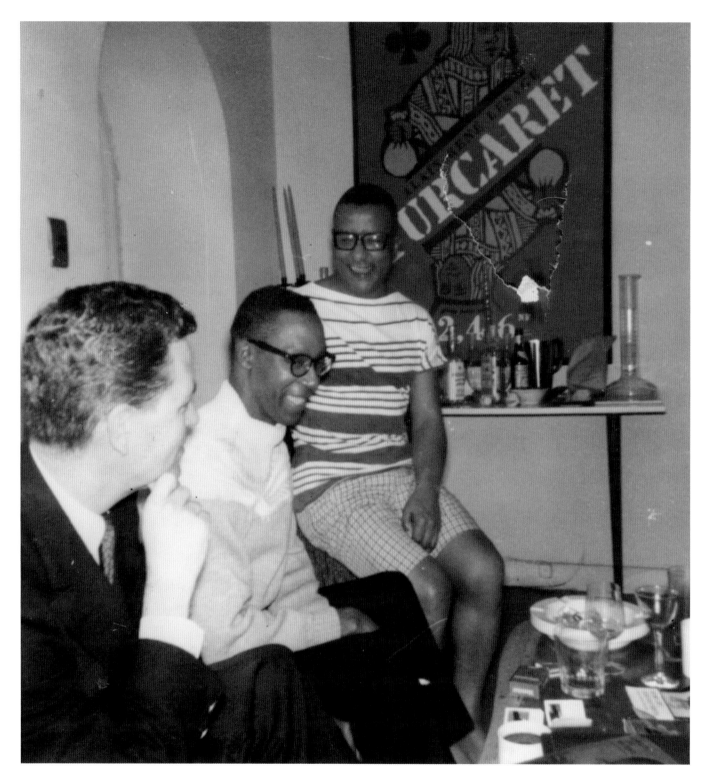

Drinks with friends at home. Bill Grove (left) and Frank Goldberg. As Billy's lover, Francis wanted to be accepted for membership in the Copasetics. His twin, Frank, came along to avoid hints of favoritism. Frank produced the "souvenir booklet" for the annual September benefit.

DONALD SHIRLEY

PIANIST

I knew Billy very, very well and heard him play many times, including once with Lena Horne at the Chez Paree in Chicago. Billy was very intuitive and knew what the occasion was. When he played with Lena Horne, he was the best possible accompanist for Lena Horne, just as when he worked with the Duke Ellington Orchestra, he performed that function perfectly. A serious musician knows that you don't play Chopin like you play Liszt, and you don't play Liszt like you play Stravinsky. Billy knew that, and that's the way he approached his duties as a musician. Billy had built into him this unique ability to adjust. One of the things that he used to say—one of his favorite phrases—was "the ability to adjust." And he was very adept at that.

And yet in his compositions, he never compromised. He was a highly skilled composer and a man of exceptional intellectual curiosity. The intellectual curiosity of creative people is always present. It isn't something that one elects to do. It is something one must do in order to exist. Billy had that.

Many composers in jazz are very good at thinking vertically and horizontally about music. But Billy could write diagonals and curves and circles, if he wanted to.

Billy was a master craftsman and pragmatic but also a romanticist. He had no personal ambition other than to see beauty thrive.

As told to David Hajdu

Even before the Copasetics was established, LeRoy, Honi, Pete, and I used to socialize with him quite a bit. It never mattered to us that Stray was gay because we had other friends who were, too. It was just no big deal. As a matter of fact, it never really came up.[57]

Atkins also discussed this important point with Hajdu:

I think the reason Strayhorn was so dedicated to the Copasetics was that he recognized how much love was in the Copasetics for him. Most people shunned people like him for being how he was, and here was a bunch of guys who were crazy about him—not because of his lifestyle or anything but for him, as a person. We made him our leader.[58]

Personal friendships blossomed into deeper connections. Coles took on the role of parental figure; Billy even called him "Father."[59] Goldberg became his spouse, and Cook became a lover.

Twelve years after Billy's death, the thirtieth anniversary annual Copasetics show of 1979 featured Cook dancing to "Take the 'A' Train" center stage. Caila Abedon watched a rehearsal and recorded a revealing and moving quote in *New York Magazine* (May 21, 1979):

The afternoon sun strikes the gold cross Cookie wears around his neck. It belonged to Billy Strayhorn, the composer of "'A' Train" and the last president of the Copasetics. . . .

"Strayhorn was the greatest friend I ever had," Cookie says, wiping his face on a towel. "When Strayhorn had a place uptown, sometimes you'd go and stay for days. Go to work if you had to and come back. You'd do your thing and I'd do mine—cooking, eating, dancing, and making

"SATIN DOLL" (1953)

It is strange how some of a composer's most famous pieces can be anomalies in his or her oeuvre. Neither Ellington nor Strayhorn hardly ever wrote straightforward Tin Pan Alley–type tunes, such as "Satin Doll." In fact, they hardly ever cowrote single works to begin with. In the case of "Satin Doll," however, Strayhorn reportedly fleshed out an Ellington riff, added chords and lyrics, and dedicated the piece to his mother, whom he lovingly called satin doll. Ellington maintained that it was his father's nickname for Evie Ellis, the unofficial Mrs. Ellington. Other women since have claimed that Duke told them that they were the song's secret dedicatee.

The tune became a modest hit in 1953 as an instrumental piece, but its success grew after Johnny Mercer added the hip lyrics. Strayhorn's original lyrics are lost, but Mercer's version may partly retain them. The Ellington sketch and the original Strayhorn reworking haven't surfaced either. There is, however, a little allusion to "Satin Doll" in Strayhorn's "Kissing Bug," composed roughly ten years earlier. The true extent of all these various contributions remains clouded—enough so that some parties took the case to court, where a judge ruled that the credits should remain as they were.

—Walter van de Leur

RECOMMENDED RECORDING

○ Anita O'Day, *My Ship* (Emily Records 1975)

---

music. Everyone sleeping together. There was nothing wrong in it. We had fun. And we had lust." He pauses. "It was gorgeous." He shakes his head hard. "It was just gorgeous."

Billy and Goldie's live-in arrangement was not characterized by the harmony and joy of his time with Bridgers. Goldberg's possessiveness and Billy's professional travel caused friction that erupted into public outbursts. Hajdu described the breakup that came in late 1959, beginning with a quote from friend Talley Beatty:

"Billy couldn't take any more shit from Goldie anymore. That was it," said Beatty. "Goldie didn't have to do it that way. He found some young boy and carried on behind Billy's back but arranged it so Billy would find him out. Little hints and weak excuses, bad lies. He was just hurting him. Goldie really knew how to be hurtful." Before Thanksgiving, Goldberg moved out of the apartment. He took most of the kitchen supplies, a painting by Felrath Hines, and the contents of the liquor cabinet.[60]

Strayhorn's final significant romantic relationship came near the end of his life. Bill Grove (William H.) trained at the Art Institute of Chicago and came initially to New York for the World's Fair of 1939.[61] A number of Grove's fellow students from the institute eventually landed in Manhattan too: Charles Sebree, Charles W. White, William McBride, John Carlis, and most significantly, Frank W Neal.[62]

Neal won a first prize scholarship in painting at the institute, but he also trained as a dancer: first with *impresaria* Sadie Bruce Glover, then with Ruth Page at the Chicago Civic Opera Ballet, and finally with Katherine Dunham, Page's assistant at this early point in her illustrious career.[63]

"The basic pattern of Ellington composing today, however, is self-control, musical certainty, knowledge of what is being done, what can be done in music. Billy Strayhorn can be credited for bringing much of this certainty into Ellington's life." *Barry Ulanov*, 1946.

Billy posing and pointing at the Unisphere, New York World's Fair, held April–October 1964 and the same months in 1965. The theme of the exhibition was "Peace Through Understanding."

Expert eyes review new compositions: Billy, sister Georgia, mother Lillian, and the Duke.

"LOVE HAS PASSED ME BY AGAIN" (1954)

In the 1950s, Strayhorn became involved with a handful of small-scale theater productions. One was based on Federico García Lorca's play *The Love of Don Perlimplín and Belisa in the Garden*, and another was a project with his friend, the composer-arranger Luther Henderson. "One of the things we talked about was looking at the world through rose-colored glasses," Henderson told Strayhorn's biographer, David Hajdu. "So we decided that that would be our theme. What's reality? What's perception? What's the difference? And what does love mean with this going on? And we called the thing *Rose-Colored Glasses*." The two never completed the show, which did not develop beyond some hip sketches set in the boppish Land of Ool-Ya-Coo.

Strayhorn wrote some compelling songs, such as the catchy "Still in Love with You," the playful "Oo (You Make Me Tingle)" (recorded by Allan Harris), and the beautiful ballad "Love Has Passed Me By Again." The lyrics are pure Strayhorn—smart and bittersweet: "Love has passed me by again / Don't ask me why / I simply cannot tell you / How love could pass me by again / And cast me in the role of Romeo at large."

—*Walter van de Leur*

RECOMMENDED RECORDING

● Allan Harris, *Love Came: The Songs of Strayhorn* (Love Records 2001)

STRAYHORN'S METHODS FOR WORKING WITH THE MAESTRO AND DEALING WITH DEADLINES

While there is much speculation on the specifics of how Strayhorn and Ellington collaborated, footage on our cutting-room floor provides insight into their unconventional methods.

Clark Terry: We were doing the movie *Anatomy of a Murder*. Duke was in Hollywood in this apartment with papers and music all over the floor. Duke was working on the score and reached a point where he had to decide whether to go to the "B" section (Clark sings it) or to the "C" section (Clark sings it). So Duke makes a long-distance phone call to New York.

He said, "Hey, Strays."

"Yes, Edward?"

"I need your expertise. I don't know whether to go to 'B' (vocalizing) or to 'C' (vocalizing) on this particular part. What would you do, Strays?"

Billy pondered for a minute. "Well, Edward, you can solve that mystery much more quickly than I can. So I think I'll leave that up to you."

Then Ellington, being the old fox that he is, kept quiet. Then Strays said, "However, if I were forced to make a decision, I would go to the 'B' (vocalizing)."

Duke said, "Okay, Strays. Thank you."

That's the way they played games with one another. But they were beautifully respectful of each other.

Luther Henderson: There's a show I worked on that was written by Duke Ellington. But Ellington couldn't devote himself to the extended time that a composer usually spends on a theatrical show, which could be six, eight, sometimes twelve weeks at times.

So Strayhorn was designated to write it, and I did some of the orchestrations under Strayhorn's direction. The show was *Beggar's Holiday*. There was a completely integrated cast, which was a first for Broadway. But the show was scored by an absentee composer because Ellington was rarely there, but Strayhorn was—all the time.

We'd gotten to a point where a ballet was needed. Strayhorn and I had adjoining rooms, and

---

Dunham was to become the matron of black American modern dance, but when Neal first met her she was also studying anthropology at the University of Chicago. On Saturday nights she gathered a broad circle of young socially aware artists at her home where the "New Negro" as envisioned by Alain Locke was a common topic. Neal was a part of that group. After Dunham's graduation and increasing travel away from Chicago (she moved to New York in 1939), Neal continued her tradition. The Neal group met at the home of Charles M. Thompson, uncle of Dorcas Pearson, Neal's wife. The couple lived with Thompson after their marriage.[64] The Neal salon in Chicago included author Richard Wright, composer Margaret Bonds, soprano

Etta Moten, poet Gwendolyn Brooks, and a number of Neal's painter, designer, and theater colleagues.

Neal's obituaries in *New York Amsterdam News* (May 14, 1955) and *Variety* (May 11, 1955) indicate that he was an "original member of Katherine Dunham's dance troupe," but he continued to be active in art, dance, and theater circles in Chicago until at least 1942. Through his involvement with the Dunham dancers, he became close to star duo Talley Beatty and Janet Collins. There too he met Dorcas Pearson, who became his wife on May 11, 1940. Family records indicate their first daughter, Sharon Woodard Neal, was born in Chicago on July 12, 1942. The young family moved to New York shortly thereafter.[65]

early in the morning, between 1:00 and 2:00 a.m., the phone rang. It was Ellington. And I could hear Strayhorn saying, "Yes, Edward. Yes. Yes," and they talked for about an hour. Strayhorn then wrote. The next day we had the "Boll Weevil Ballet." It's a collaboration the likes of which I doubt seriously ever has or ever will be seen again.

Herb Jordan: Duke, from the very first time that he heard Billy Strayhorn, understood that he could learn from Billy Strayhorn, and Duke was brilliant that way: one of his gifts was to identify talent and to learn from it. It's one of the things that made their collaboration so great; they made one another better.

Don Shirley: Billy always worked under pressure. Billy would wait until the last minute to do whatever Duke wanted him to do. If there was something that was needed on a Wednesday, Billy didn't get started on it until Tuesday night, with a bottle of Scotch or something. But he would always complete it. He'd get it done. He liked working under pressure!

CT: We were doing an album called *Blue Rose* with Rosemary Clooney. We started to record it in New York with the band. But Rosie was pregnant and had to stay in California, and we had a deadline.

So we finished the sound track, left room for Rosie's spaces and openings. Strayhorn took the sound track, got on a plane, and went to California.

Rosie overdubbed everything and did it beautifully with Strayhorn's coaching. There's hardly any inkling that it was dubbed that way. I don't think anybody could detect it. I can't say for sure, but it had to be one of the first times an album was ever made that way.

Strayhorn was the type of person who, regardless of how hurried or scurried you might be in getting a project done, would walk in and calmly say in so many words, "Relax. Let's do it." And he would get it done. There was no such thing as a deadline for him because he just did the project leisurely and relaxed and beautifully, efficiently, and correctly, until it was finished.

Strays had his own way of doing things. That's one of the very important factors for Ellington, because he knew Strays was going to do it Strays' way. And Strays' way was all right for Ellington's way. So in fact they became a highway, the both of them together.

—Robert Levi

Writer Carol J. Oja dates the beginning of the Neal salon in New York as "some point in the 1940s" and David Hajdu places Strayhorn's association with it beginning "shortly after his return from Paris in 1950." The group met at 10 West Twenty-Eighth Street in a "moderate sized second-floor space with wide windows that overlooked a row of storefronts; a view without charm, it turned the eye inward." [66] Dorcas Neal said:

I guess you could say this was a safe place to be. It was a safe place for a group of people who were just different to be in the company of those who were the same. It was all like a family situation. This was a breeding ground for a certain group of artists at a certain time when they had nowhere else to go. It was like Bloomsbury.[67] In this group, these people could be the artists they were and be dealt with like artists. They all faced a lot of the same problems and a lot of the same questions regarding their careers and their place in the world, which really was a white world at the time. Together, I think they were able to answer many of those questions for each other and solve those problems and become successful in the world. . . . Really, the group were mostly people who were black and gay—but not everybody, mind you.[68]

Bill Coleman was an intimate Strayhorn friend in New York from the earliest days of the Strayhorn/Bridgers circle, to the salon-style gatherings at the homes of the Neals and the Logans. He stood by Billy through his final illness and celebrated his life afterward. He said of his friend, "He was very strong and had an extraordinary capacity to absorb things that would be devastating to someone else and carry on."

In addition to the Neals, Strayhorn, and Grove, the salon included Talley Beatty, Felrath Hines, and Charles Sebree from Chicago. Others, from New York, included Arthur Smith (a jewelry maker friend of Sebree's), Eartha Kitt (a Dunham dancer), James Baldwin ("when he was in the city"), singers Harry Belafonte and Brock Peters, composers John Cage and Lou Harrison, and Strayhorn friends Lena Horne and Bill Coleman. Dorcas recalled that Billy was "very active" and that "it was a big shot in the arm for him at that time."[69] Of Grove, Dorcas said, "There weren't a lot of white faces in the lot, but he was one of them. Grove didn't mind at all. You might say he liked it."[70]

On Mother's Day May 9, 1955, the car Frank Neal was driving on wet pavement skidded off the Grand Central Parkway and struck a light pole. He died the following morning.[71] Dorcas continued to be Strayhorn's friend, becoming part of the Logan circle in the '60s.[72]

In 1965, the friendship Grove and Strayhorn had enjoyed at the Neal and Logan homes blossomed into a blissful, supportive relationship that, in combination with the vigils held by Strayhorn's family members and friends, saw Billy past the portal.

[They] kept separate apartments, but as Strayhorn grew more seriously ill, they were rarely seen apart. . . . Grove joined Strayhorn at the Copasetics meetings, a de facto member. . . . It was Strayhorn and Grove at the Logans' ("He sat and kept quiet, but he was there—and Martin [King] liked him. He gave a bunch of big checks," said Marian Logan). . . . On a summer weekend in 1966, Strayhorn brought Grove around to meet his brothers. . . . Every weekend, as a rule, Strayhorn and Grove called a limo and took a ride out of Manhattan, sometimes with friends, including Dwike Mitchell. . . . Strayhorn and Grove spent

LINER NOTES

"BALLAD FOR VERY TIRED AND VERY SAD LOTUS EATERS" (1956)

Both Duke Ellington and Billy Strayhorn had a very close musical rapport with Johnny Hodges, who was undoubtedly one of the main assets of the Ellington orchestra. Hodges was featured in many ballads that were tailored to his stellar command of the alto saxophone. He combined his creamy tone, impeccable diction, and stunning glissandi with a deep understanding of the music he played. His playing was never sentimental, and he never lost himself in effects. In fact, Hodges would stay virtually motionless and seemingly unaffected while performing some of those great ballads written especially for him, and he kept a safe distance from all-too-teary renditions. That made him an excellent spokesman for Strayhorn's music and, not surprisingly, the soloist whom Strayhorn featured the most.

Strayhorn composed the beautifully eloquent and soft-spoken "Ballad for Very Tired and Very Sad Lotus Eaters" for Johnny Hodges and a small ensemble, and it was recorded with the composer at the piano. As with so many of his ballads, Strayhorn paired this beautiful and somewhat mysterious melody with a highly sophisticated harmonic progression. (For Strayhorn connoisseurs, the passage in the second bar will be familiar: he used the same chord in the fifth bar of "U.M.M.G.," as well as in the entire theme of "Cashmere Cutie.") Whatever those lotus eaters had been going through, this song must certainly have soothed them. This little-known composition is a gem.

—Walter van de Leur

RECOMMENDED RECORDING

○ Johnny Hodges and the Ellington All-Stars, *Duke's in Bed* (Verve 1956)

Billy and Bill
Grove on
St. Vincent,
December
1966.

154

Billy gathering souvenirs from a local artisan and merchant in St. Vincent. Handcrafted bags and carved wooden bowls are visible in the shop. Billy's eating device, a necessity of his cancer treatment, is mostly covered by his shirt.

With Marian Bruce Logan (right) and an unidentified woman. Probably on St. Vincent at the end of 1966.

At New Year's 1967 Billy had just returned from a trip to St. Vincent with Bill Grove and the Logan family. He wrote a note to friends in gratitude for their support during his illness.

May the new Year be as good to you as you were kind to me during my illness

Billy Strayhorn

In the days between Christmas 1966 and New Year's 1967 "Dear Arturo" (Logan) and "Itty Bitty Buddy" (Strayhorn) enjoyed a final vacation together. They spent it with Marian Bruce Logan, Chip Logan (Billy's godson), and Bill Grove on the island of St. Vincent in the Caribbean.

the eight days from Christmas 1966 through New Year's Day 1967 with the Logans (including their three-and-a-half-year-old son Chip, Strayhorn's godson) on St. Vincent, in the Caribbean. . . . With Bill Grove's help, Strayhorn held on. He had the walls of his apartment repainted in light, bright colors, and Grove hung a set of sheer, pale yellow curtains, as if to magnify the sunlight. . . . Every evening, Bill Grove took the commuter train from Mount Vernon to the 125th Street stop and walked directly to the Hospital for Joint Diseases. . . . A little past halfway to dawn, at 4:45 a.m. on May 31, 1967, Billy Strayhorn died of esophageal cancer at the age of fifty-one. Bill Grove was with him.[73]

That Grove was present with Strayhorn at his death shows remarkable determination, given hospital regulations that prohibited a gay partner from remaining at his bedside.

Did Billy Strayhorn Sell His Soul?

Writer Adam Gopnik referred to Billy as "adopted" and "infantilized," and those are kind versions of what he implied as Ellington's strength and Billy's weakness.[74] At Strayhorn's centennial, what can be said about the depiction of him as a meek homosexual pawn of the super-macho Duke? Did he tolerate anonymity as the price of a chance to live his queer life openly in an era, an ethnic group, and a musical culture that would have squashed him if he had attempted to grasp for equality? Was he a little man whose mannerisms betrayed him (better stay hidden) just as clearly as did the color of his skin? Did self-effacement eat away at his soul, drowning the validation of his genius in alcohol and burning up his life in puffs of smoke from the cigarettes he craved in every waking moment?

His family medical and social history is pertinent: only one of his five siblings who reached adulthood

"UPPER MANHATTAN MEDICAL GROUP" (1956)

In the late 1940s, Strayhorn joined a group of tap-dance professionals who named themselves the Copasetics. For the next decade or so, Strayhorn wrote music for their annual shows. Before long, they made him their president, even though he wasn't a hoofer himself. But there was a rhythmic kinship. "Listen to some of the figures in Strayhorn's pieces, like 'U.M.M.G.,' those are dances—tap dances maybe. . . . [Y]ou can dance with a lot of things besides your feet. Billy Strayhorn was . . . [a] dancer—in his mind. He was a dance-writer," Ellington wrote.

Written in dedication to Dr. Arthur Logan, the personal physician of both Strayhorn and Ellington, "Upper Manhattan Medical Group" (usually referred to as "U.M.M.G.") is an outspokenly boppish piece. Still, it is fully in concordance with the general developments in Strayhorn's oeuvre at the time. Even without the emergence of bebop, Strayhorn still might have written works such as "U.M.M.G." If indeed he had been borrowing certain techniques from the younger jazz generation, by no means was it at the expense of his own voice.

—Walter van de Leur

RECOMMENDED RECORDING

◉ Branford Marsalis, *Trio Jeepy* (Columbia 1989)

Organized in 1939 by Dr. George Dows Cannon and based on the Mayo Clinic model, the Upper Manhattan Medical Group was one of the first group practices in the nation. In 1959, thirty-four doctors served seventeen thousand patients. Both Arthur Logan (seated in the front row, fourth from right) and his sister Myra Adele Logan (second from right) were founding members. Billy's tribute song, "U.M.M.G.," was written for Ellington's West Coast tour in 1954 and first recorded in 1956. Billy included the piece in his New College concert (1965) and played on the subsequent recording.

Billy paid a bill for cancer treatment to his friend and charter member of the U.M.M.G., Dr. Arthur Logan. The building at 1865 Amsterdam Avenue is now occupied by a Family Health Center and Urgent Care practice.

lived until their seventieth birthday—the youngest, Lillian; his sister Georgia died at age fifty-three from emphysema; Theodore, unmarried like Billy, died at age fifty-three from esophageal cancer; John died at fifty-six; and Jimmy died at sixty-four.[75] Patterns of susceptibility to alcoholism were manifest in his family, and they were smokers in a time when most of America was too. A person with a cocktail in one hand and a cigarette in the other was "sophisticated." (One who could manage both in the same hand was even more so.) Billy's death at fifty-one in itself, even acknowledging his drinking and smoking as specific causes, does not mark him as self-loathing.

Duke Ellington died from lung cancer, and many others in the band were also taken by diseases caused by addiction. Secondhand smoke blown in one another's face on Ellington's train cars alone likely contributed to the early deaths of many of them. Ivie Anderson, for example, died from asthma at age forty-four. In the past one hundred years, how many black men, jazz musicians—artists of any color, stripe, or hue—died by age fifty-one? How many of them would have traded their genius for a comfortable life in the shadow of another (perhaps lesser) man?

What was the role of Joe Morgen in downplaying Billy's significance in the Ellington phenomenon? Ellington hired Morgen as his publicity manager in 1949. It is clear that from that point Morgen intentionally obscured Billy's role in "the Ellington Effect." Morgen was totally devoted to negating anyone or

SUCH SWEET THUNDER: "THE STAR-CROSSED LOVERS" (AKA "PRETTY GIRL"), "UP AND DOWN, UP AND DOWN," AND "HALF THE FUN" (1956–1957)

In 1956 Ellington and Strayhorn were developing ideas for a suite that celebrated the music of "the Bard of Avon," which they called the *Shakespearean Suite*. Strayhorn decided to brush up on Shakespeare, and he first reread *A Midsummer Night's Dream*. This comic play provided him with the suite's title, *Such Sweet Thunder*, and resulted in the intricate "Up and Down, Up and Down." The work portrays the mischievous elf Robin Goodfellow, also known as Puck, who confuses the play's lovers: "Up and down, up and down / I will lead them up and down." Two groups of instruments depict the various couples, which Puck mixes up. The resultant interplay shows off Strayhorn's smart, polyphonic, and multi-linear writing. Trumpeter Clark Terry closes with Shakespeare's famous, "Lord, what fools these mortals be!"

When Ellington decided to premiere the suite much earlier than initially planned, Strayhorn had to cut corners. He adapted two earlier compositions that, under new titles, fit the suite's motif. The breathtaking "Pretty Girl" became "The Star-Crossed Lovers," portraying Romeo and Juliet, and the subdued "Lately" served as movement eleven, retitled "Half the Fun." The other movements are by Ellington and are arguably among his best compositions.

—*Walter van de Leur*

RECOMMENDED RECORDING

○ Duke Ellington and His Orchestra, *Such Sweet Thunder* (Columbia 1957)

Billy praised Duke's teaching prowess, not so much for ability to provide explicit instruction, but for the trust he placed in his collaborators and the extraordinary results that came from trusting the right people.

Handshake with the Duke. From left: Pianists Aaron Bridgers and Marian McPartland, [person unknown], Ellington, Strayhorn, trumpeter Harold "Shorty" Baker, and [person unknown].

ON THE CHALLENGES OF BEING OPENLY GAY

Fred Hersch: In the 1940s and 1950s, gay people were not out in any way. The Motion Picture Production Code stipulated that if anybody was gay or immoral in a film they had to die—they had to be killed. If you loved somebody of the same sex, you were doomed in film.

Mercedes Ellington: It was very dangerous then to be a homosexual—male or female—it was like the kiss of death. That's why it took movie stars so long to come out of the closet, and it continued on to the '60s, '70s, '80s, and '90s.

Terell Stafford: I can't imagine being a gay African American during those times because the jazz community was extremely homophobic; to this day, it hasn't really changed, and that's unfortunate. You see how the music has progressed, but that mentality has not.

Herb Jordan: Billy Strayhorn was one of the few artists of his era who was willing to be open with his homosexuality. If you consider the times, you know it was common practice for gay actors and gay composers to associate themselves with women to disguise their homosexuality. Strayhorn exhibited strength of character in that he was very confident with who he was, and everyone understood that if you dealt with Billy Strayhorn you had to accept him as he was or not at all, and that again was revolutionary for that period.

—Robert Levi

anything that might challenge the superiority of Ellington's image. He was also a homophobe who specifically disliked Billy. The most egregious evidence of his antipathy was the story Morgen concocted and distributed after Billy's death:

> Billy, who remained a bachelor until death, leaves as a legacy his views on bachelorhood in an exclusive interview before his death. Said Billy:

"Ellington's so apt explanation of his own feelings about women, 'I love them madly,' had a bell-like echo of beautiful truth for me, too. Only in my case I really love them ALL—madly. In so doing in band business here, there and mostly everywhere, year in, year out, I've found simply I get along much better emphasizing the 'all.'

"Do not, please, get me wrong. I certainly have nothing against the time-honored institution of

"CASHMERE CUTIE" (1957)

In 1957, Duke Ellington's publishing company Tempo Music filed a copyright in the name of Billy Strayhorn for "Cashmere Cutie." These were the years when the Ellington orchestra was bouncing back from times of hardship suffered during the early 1950s, and both Ellington and Strayhorn were in the midst of one of their most creative postwar periods. Strayhorn had just finished his work for a number of ambitious projects with the Ellington orchestra: sessions with singers Rosemary Clooney (1956) and Ella Fitzgerald (1957); the *Ellington Indigos* LP (1957), for which he wrote practically all the arrangements; and some collaborative efforts with Ellington such as the television play *A Drum Is a Woman* (1956) and the Shakespeare-inspired suite *Such Sweet Thunder* (1957).

On top of all that musical activity, Strayhorn found time to write works such as "Cashmere Cutie," which apparently didn't fill a need in the orchestra's band book. The band may have played it, but Ellington never took the work into the recording studio. As trumpeter Clark Terry once recalled, the band could be playing a one-nighter in a small town and Ellington would bring out a new work "especially composed for the occasion." They would sight-read it on the spot, and after that one performance the band would never get to play the piece again.

Undoubtedly, there were many Strayhorn works among these tryouts. Envelopes in the Duke Ellington Collection reveal that Strayhorn mailed Ellington his latest work if the orchestra was on the road. In the case of "Cashmere Cutie," it is barely forgivable that the finest of all jazz orchestras passed on the chance to record this superb composition, which is so full of Eastern flavors that it could easily have been included in *The Far East Suite*, the last truly brilliant Ellington-Strayhorn collaboration.

If anything, "Cashmere Cutie" is genuine Strayhorn. Underneath its attractive melody, which evokes a mystical world on a far and distant shore, lies an intricate harmonic structure and an irregular form. The cross-section voicings, the rhythmically challenging brass backgrounds, the surprising melodic displacement in the final chorus, and the overall sense of balance and musical logic all illustrate Billy Strayhorn's impressive talent.

—Walter van de Leur

RECOMMENDED RECORDING

⊙ Dutch Jazz Orchestra, *Portrait of a Silk Thread: Newly Discovered Works of Billy Strayhorn* (Challenge 1995)

"BLUES IN ORBIT" (1958)

With the hectic recording schedule of the second half of the 1950s, Strayhorn often wrote bluesy and riff-based compositions—pieces that could be written swiftly. They mainly served as a backdrop for improvisations by the orchestra's star soloists. In addition, the swinging blues undoubtedly went over well with the audience and band members alike: their artistry notwithstanding, the Ellingtonians could be surprisingly undemanding when it came to their own musical preferences. Johnny Hodges, for one, recorded many straightforward blues songs under his own steam. Reportedly, his 1950 departure from Ellington was partly fueled by the orchestra's more ambitious repertoire: "We didn't like the tone poems much," he said.

The list of Strayhorn compositions based on the blues is significant: "Festival Junction" and "Blues to Be There" (both *Newport Jazz Festival Suite*), *BDB* (for the album with the combined Basie and Ellington orchestras), "Blues I + II" (recorded as "Blues" on *Duke Ellington Presents . . .*), "Beyond Category" and "The E and D Blues" (patches for the *Songbook* recordings), "Sweet and Pungent" (*Blues in Orbit* album), "Tymperturbably Blue" (*Jazz Party*), and other various titles recorded at stockpile sessions ("Cordon Bleu," "Rod La Roque," "Frère Monk," "Blousons Noirs").

These blues-based works often carried Strayhorn's characteristic melodic and harmonic turns and, most notably, his recognizable orchestrations. In "Blues in Orbit" (from the album by the same name), originally titled "Star Blues," Strayhorn calls upon trumpeter Clark Terry to lead the reeds—a method he had used before. The music seems almost frozen in space, and without any clear introduction or coda, there are more questions than answers.

—*Walter van de Leur*

RECOMMENDED RECORDING

Duke Ellington and His Orchestra, *Blues in Orbit* (Columbia 1960)

---

wedlock. Some of my dearest and sanest friends are married, come to think. But the fact remains I just don't believe marriage and Strayhorn would hit a lasting happy medium, that's all.

"Look, I'm an individualist. The rugged kind. I don't bat an eye when the fellows in the band call me a character. I know they're right. I am. I'll never foist, at that proven rate, then, the character who is Strayhorn on any man's daughter, so undeserving such fate.

"My life as arranger with the Ellington orchestra is a darn hectic one. Arrangers of a necessity travel along with their outfits. Duke follows a staggering yearly schedule of concerts, dances, recording dates, theaters, and club dates.

"Love or not, I wouldn't subject a wife to the road. It's punishment. Often I work around the clock scoring the exacting music for Ellington. I've gone days without shaving. Kept awake with coffee, cigarettes and chewed pencil tips. I snarl at little children. I'm not fit company for man nor beast. The chosen Eve of my life surely has no reason to put up with that cross-section.

"I'm an impulsive guy, what's more. I feel no pain if, say in Los Angeles, I get an urge to work at the piano in my New York apartment then spend

Billy loved Paris. From his early lyrics for "Lush Life" to visits with Bridgers, to work with Orson Welles (*The Blessed and the Damned*) and Sam Shaw (*Paris Blues*), to his private recording of *The Peaceful Side* (1961), the city always "eased the bite of it." The photo captures him looking wistfully from behind a wall at Versailles, outside his beloved city.

Photograph from the collection of pianist Marian McPartland. She played regularly at Hickory House, her set including a rendition of "Lush Life." Hajdu chronicles that Strayhorn would turn to face her at the end of her performance, raise his cocktail in a toast, and proclaim, "Aaaah!"

the early morning hours with friends in a favorite bar in Greenwich Village. I'll be on a New York bound plane in a few hours, asleep and content. That's my life and I want it to stay that way. Pressure of domestic routine and patterns of responsibility are just not my dish. I like disorder. Many of my friends are absolutely mad. My apartment may get a thorough cleaning and it may not. Stan Kenton or Lena and Lennie or Marie Bryant with an Indian maharajah may run by tonight and find their highball glasses where they left them last week.

"And money. That's the stuff I'm mostly without most of the time. What practical woman would laugh gaily and tell me, oh, to forget it? If she did she would be more a character than I and would I want or need that? Yes, about like a hole in the head.

"I was quite impressed with the unmarried women I met in France and Italy. They absolutely fascinated me. They know (and use) the art of making a man think he's the most wonderful object on earth today. I had to make no apology nor offer explanation of my single status. More than once in Paris I heard a feminine voice say, 'C'est la vie (That's life), Beel!' It sure is."[76]

THE NUTCRACKER SUITE (1960)

By arranging Tchaikovsky's *The Nutcracker Suite*, an excerpt from the full *Nutcracker Ballet*, Strayhorn and Ellington stepped into a jazz tradition that stemmed from the earliest years when ragtime piano players were "ragging the classics." As usual, the composers divided the work at hand between the two of them, and as usual, Strayhorn ended up arranging the lion's share: "Overture," "Toot Toot Tootie Toot," "Sugar Rum Cherry," "Entr'acte," "Dance of the Floreadores," and "Arabesque Cookie" are his adaptations. Ellington did "Peanut Brittle Brigade." It is unclear who arranged "The Volga Vouty" and "Chinoiserie."

The *Jazz-Nutcracker*, as the suite became known, is a triumph in its lucid adaptation of Pyotr Ilyich Tchaikovsky's orchestral score. Instead of simply jazzing up the suite, Strayhorn (and Ellington) virtually recomposed the ballet, taking it to a new and highly personal level.

The final section of the *Nutcracker Suite*, a reworking of "Arab Dance," provides an excellent illustration.

Strayhorn's playful adaptation calls for a bamboo flute over a camel-like gait played by the bass and drums. Tchaikovsky's quasi-Eastern quality is preserved but with a twist—halfway through, the band moves into a medium-swing feel that shows the orchestra's true character. Perhaps this last section of the *Jazz-Nutcracker* sums up the great virtues of the entire adaptation: Strayhorn and Ellington produced a new reading of a classical work without sacrificing their own or the original composer's music. All the other movements in the suite show a similar balance among wit, irony, and tribute.

—*Walter van de Leur*

RECOMMENDED RECORDING

◉ Duke Ellington and His Orchestra, *The Nutcracker Suite* (Columbia 1960)

JIMMY WOODE

BASSIST, DUKE ELLINGTON ORCHESTRA

Strayhorn was so well versed and so well informed about everything. During some of our European trips with the band, I would go off with Strayhorn to side places. He was so well informed about this historical thing there and that thing there. He was a very well versed and learned person but so self-effacing. And what a gentleman! What a prince—really a prince. I've never heard one person say one negative word about Billy Strayhorn.

He was also a fashion plate—but a very self-styled fashion plate. We went shopping, but he was not only interested in clothes; he was also a gourmand—not a gourmet but a gourmand. And he was interested in styles of furniture, different periods of styles of furniture. I never asked him how he came to know so much or how he was so well informed, but he was.

I've always had a feeling that from the time that his association with Ellington started, a lot of Strayhorn's qualities rubbed off on Ellington. As I would listen to Ellington speak, I would think, "Oh, one minute now. That's a quote from Strayhorn. That originated with Strayhorn." I observed these two gentlemen very closely, and I feel that Strayhorn not only contributed a lot to the music of Duke Ellington but also to his way of thinking about life and living. I think he gave a lot to Ellington.

Previous to his passing on, he was very angry. We sat in Paris at the Living Room, where Aaron Bridgers played, for a very early breakfast, because we had been out all night. And he was angry. He said, "Why me, Jamie? Why not some of those gangsters?" He said, "I've just begun to write. I've just begun to live."

As told to David Hajdu

Billy Strayhorn shaking hands with Willie "The Lion" Smith, with Janie Smith on right, during a jazz workshop at the Pittsburgh Jazz Festival, June 1965. As a primary influence on Duke Ellington, Willie "The Lion" Smith was Strayhorn's jazz grandfather. *Photograph by Charles "Teenie" Harris, American, 1908–1998, Kodak Safety Film, H: 4 in. x W: 5 in., Carnegie Museum of Art, Pittsburgh, Heinz Family Fund.*

THE FAR EAST SUITE: "BLUEBIRD OF DELHI," "ISFAHAN," AND "AGRA"
(1963-1964)

In 1964, a so-called State Department tour took the Ellington orchestra and Strayhorn to Syria, Jordan, India, Sri Lanka (then Ceylon), Pakistan, Iran (then Persia), Lebanon, and Turkey. Upon their return, Ellington and Strayhorn set out to translate their impressions of the trip into an extended work. The resultant *Far East Suite* is undoubtedly one of the highlights of the Ellington-Strayhorn collaboration, possibly because the work drew on the rich musical cultures of the Asian and Arab countries through which they had traveled. Strayhorn contributed "Bluebird of Delhi," "Isfahan," and "Agra."

"Bluebird of Delhi" depicts the singing of a bird, a mynah, which reportedly visited the balcony of his hotel room in New Delhi every day. Ellington wrote that Strayhorn "was always talking to it—'How are you today?,' 'Good morning!,' 'Do you want something to eat?'—but the bird never answered him until he was leaving the room and Delhi. Then it sounded off the low raspberry you hear at the end of the number."

"Isfahan," named after (then) Persia's former capital, was actually composed as "Elf" months before the beginning of the trip. Like pieces such as "Pretty Girl," "Passion Flower," "A Flower Is a Lovesome Thing," "Rod La Roque," and "Blood Count," it was tailor-made for altoist Johnny Hodges, with whom Strayhorn had a close musical rapport. The piece is loved by musicians all over the world, and it has been recorded in hundreds of different versions.

The Taj Mahal in the Indian city of Agra was one of the obvious stops for the Ellingtonians, and the white marble building sufficiently impressed Strayhorn to dedicate a piece to the tomb and its legend, titled "Agra." The marble construction has been said to be "designed by giants and finished by jewelers"—an apt description of the building, the baritone saxophonist, and Strayhorn's composition.

—Walter van de Leur

RECOMMENDED RECORDING

○ Duke Ellington and His Orchestra, *The Far East Suite* (Columbia 1967)

No one other than Morgen could have made up such a ridiculous scenario, and nothing could be less like Billy Strayhorn than the person there portrayed. This is the same Billy who said to Dorcas Neal: "I'm not going to change for anybody, and if they don't like it, that's their problem"?[77]

Was Billy's sexuality the primary factor in his "willingness" to accept an anonymous role? There is no evidence Billy ever attempted to hide his sexuality from Ellington, anyone in the Ellington organization, or anybody else. The lyrics of songs he wrote before meeting Duke—in fact two of the songs that legend has it he presented to Ellington in their first meeting—are to be read as aspirations of a gay man ("Something to Live For") and apprehensions about a future spent alone ("Life Is Lonely," aka "Lush Life").[78] Weight for this conclusion does not rest on the presence of the word "gay" in both songs, though it is there. Dismissal of the subject based on whether the word would have carried the denotation to Billy and his circle in

APPRECIATION

Dianne Reeves: His music lives on. We're speaking about Billy Strayhorn because we're still discovering his treasures. Had he lived longer, he would still be writing all of this wonderful music, and there would have been a great community of people that would have embraced him.

Alyce Claerbaut: I'm so passionate about this because Billy Strayhorn's life is a life that mattered. He mattered because he contributed so much to our culture and to our history.

Nancy Wilson: There's nothing more classy than "Lush Life." I wish he would have written more, but "Lush Life" I'd have to rank up there with one of the greatest songs that has ever been written. So, yes, I'd put Billy Strayhorn up there with Gershwin and Porter.

Luther Henderson: Strayhorn was also a great lyricist. His imagery was unique and wonderful. I suspect that left on his own, writing for the theater might have become his thing because he wrote lyrics and words. He was a kind of combination like Cole Porter or Irving Berlin, who wrote their own lyrics and words. And with Strayhorn's intellect and knowledge of literature and his literary sensibility, he could very well have been not just a great lyricist but a great playwright and musical comedy person.

Gail Buckley (Author): For me, the legacy of Billy Strayhorn is Billy Strayhorn as a person. I've never known anyone quite like him, and I never will know anyone like him. He was not of this earth. He was so smart, such a poet and a funny man, so beautiful to look at and to listen to. He was so special. That's his legacy. I can see him right now. His face.

Jon Hendricks (Jazz Vocalist and Lyricist): The most important thing about Billy Strayhorn we don't know is that he did what George Bernard Shaw said nobody does: he practiced Christianity. He had the other cheek ready for you if you hit him on one. You ask him for his shirt, he had two to give you. You ask him to go one mile with you, he'd go ten. He practiced Christianity. And a person who does that becomes almost invisible, because as George Bernard Shaw says, the only thing wrong with Christianity is nobody practices it.

Chico Hamilton: I sincerely hope the world is able to see how beautiful Swee' Pea really is because he's still here. Anytime you listen to one of his tunes, he's here. Like he said, "My eye is watching the noon crowd." It's cool, right? "My eye is watching the noon crowd." Hell of a lyric, man, "because I've got something to live for." That's it!

—Robert Levi

the 1930s that it now does is to miss the wider context of both songs.

Ellington said that in their first meeting he was impressed with two things: Billy's lyrics (!) and his laughter. Billy's personal demeanor left Ellington little doubt as to his orientation. Hajdu cites boyhood friend Mickey Scrima that in high school "people used to call him a sissy,"[79] and while other epithets may address "artistic sensitivity" or plain oddness, a "sissy" is one thing—effeminate. As a rising star of African American culture during the Harlem Renaissance, Ellington had certainly known members of Billy's tribe before. Clearly, that was not a sufficient issue to frighten the Duke away from forming a professional, then intensely personal, relationship with Billy over the next thirty years.

Mercer Ellington recorded incidents that show his father maintained personal ambivalence about gay men. Ranging from rants about a "Faggot Mafia" who "hired their own kind whenever they could" and

SUITE FOR THE DUO (1963/1966)

Gravely ill with cancer, Strayhorn worked with the French horn-piano duo of Willie Ruff and Dwike Mitchell on a suite that he titled *The North by Southwest Suite*. The suite consists of three movements: "Up There," "Boo Loose," and "Pavane Bleu No. 2" (pronounced *Pavane Bleu Numéro Deux*). Since Tempo Music wrongly listed "Blue Cloud" as an alternate title for both "Boo Loose" and "Blood Count," it seems that the latter was Strayhorn's final work and part of an otherwise unknown suite.

Strayhorn worked closely with Ruff and Mitchell, who recorded the suite after his death as *Suite for the Duo*.

The French horn—somber when played low, majestic in its middle register, and aggressive in its extremes—enabled Strayhorn to express the wide range of emotions that struggled to get out in the final stages of his life. As Willie Ruff noted, the work "thunders with highly autobiographical overtones; the moods of a vibrant musical career, shutting down."

—Walter van de Leur

RECOMMENDED RECORDING

◉ The Mitchell-Ruff Duo, *Strayhorn: A Mitchell-Ruff Interpretation* (1967; Kepler 2004)

---

how "when they had achieved executive status, they maneuvered to keep straight guys out of influential positions"[80] to Mercer's presumption that Duke and Billy "experimented" to reports from "cats" in the band that one of them had interrupted a sexual encounter between Ellington and Strayhorn, there must have existed some fluidity in the Duke's vaunted "sexual appetite."[81] Hajdu's article in *Vanity Fair* in 1999 included a photograph of a partly nude Billy sitting seductively in bed. That photo was found in Ellington's prayer book he carried with him and used daily. As Mercer said, "It seemed like a given." Hajdu, then president of the Duke Ellington Society, received no little grief from the publication of this article and its speculations about their relationship.

Photograph by John Miner dated May 26, 1952. Billy playing, probably in a Chicago home—the newspaper on the piano is the *Chicago Daily Sun-Times*.

Strayhorn and Jerry (Jerome) O. Rhea,
Ellington's public relations agent, secretary,
and assistant, pose with a musical score.
June 1947.

"BLOOD COUNT" (1966?)

"Blood Count" is undoubtedly one of Strayhorn's most dramatic works for the Ellington orchestra. Originally featuring Johnny Hodges—the altoist for whom Strayhorn wrote more ballads than for any other Ellingtonian—the work's sad context deepens its meaning. Strayhorn wrote "Blood Count" at a time when he was seriously ill with esophageal cancer. Reportedly, it was his final work, scored at the Hospital of Joint Diseases on Manhattan's Upper East Side. However, Strayhorn composed the piece years earlier, around 1964, when he was indeed ill but his condition did not seem terminal. As the original manuscripts reveal, Strayhorn retitled the work "Blue Cloud" in the final months of his life and made a new arrangement.

Due to a title mix-up in his publisher's catalogue, "Blood Count" has been mistaken for one of the movements of a suite that Strayhorn was working on at the time: *The North by Southwest Suite* (recorded as *Suite for the Duo*), but there is no relationship. "Blood Count" is a forceful and tormented ballad that derives its expressive powers from typical Strayhornisms: a tightly composed dramatic melody against a lean but highly effective background. Its theme seems full of interrupted thoughts, and the fatalism of the unresolved descending line in the final bars seems to explore emotions not previously heard in Strayhorn's work. "Blood Count" conjures up the devastating consequences of his progressing cancer and seems to express his feelings of sadness, frustration, and failure.

—*Walter van de Leur*

RECOMMENDED RECORDING

⊙ The Stan Getz Quartet, *Pure Getz* (Concord Jazz 1982)

It is just as reasonable, and indeed far more likely, that Billy was to Duke what his de facto "wives" were. He was married only once, to Mercer's mother, Edna Thompson (they never divorced), but he lived with Mildred Dixon for ten years, with Beatrice "Evie" Ellis from 1938 until his death, and he maintained a regular relationship with Fernanda de Castro Monte from 1960 until he died. He loved each of them deeply, provided for them financially, and drew different things from the companionship of each. From them he required absolute discretion and public silence about the nature of their relationships. Why would he not have required the same from Billy? Kalamu ya Salaam referred to them as "musically married,"[82] but there was more to it than that. There is little doubt that the "love of his life" was Billy Strayhorn—whether or not they ever were sexual companions.

There is additional evidence of the uniqueness of Duke's protection of Billy. A closeted jazz musician who knew Billy well told Hajdu:

> For those of us who were both black and homosexual in that time, acceptance was of paramount importance, absolutely paramount importance. Duke Ellington afforded Billy that acceptance. That was something that cannot be undervalued or under-appreciated. To Billy, that was gold.[83]

Hajdu concluded there were two things Billy gained through his continued association with Ellington: "a high-profile outlet for his artistry" and "emotional support."

In *Music Is My Mistress* (1973), Duke Ellington recalled of Billy, "I can still hear his voice clearly clearing up any point of indecision with his watchword: 'Ever onward and upward!' Many people are indebted to Billy Strayhorn, and I more than anybody."

Gay bars were dangerous places to be seen in the 1940s. Policemen often raided them, arrested anyone found having physical contact with someone of the same gender, jailed them, and published their names in the newspaper, leading many to lose families, jobs, and friends. Billy and Aaron more frequently entertained at home, but in this photo they enjoy a risky night out in Harlem with the boys.

Did Billy seek Ellington's approval, flourish under his nurture, and ultimately decide to remain with him even if that meant his contributions were not always fully acknowledged? Yes, he did so. Did he like it? Billy's niece Alyce Claerbaut points out:

> Strayhorn did *not* choose to be obscure. He attempted to leave Ellington on several occasions in order to pursue his own path. The myth that Strayhorn chose to remain obscure in order to live as a gay man does not make any sense. He was out about his sexuality. Why would he be closeted about his genius?[84]

As David Hill, a long-time Ellington and Strayhorn devotee puts it:

> The relationship between Billy and Duke was complex, but it is undeniable that Ellington held most of the cards in terms of how the music written for the orchestra was performed, and it is also undeniable that Duke took advantage of this relationship at times, in two ways. First, he did the same thing Irving Mills had done to him—taking partial or even full credit financially for music that he had not written. These kinds of historical inaccuracies continue to this day, forty years after Duke's death, reinforced by musicians and educators who should know better. And second, he used Billy to make up for his own shortcomings when it came to deadlines, while often taking full credit once again for these contributions.
>
> In defense of Duke, people always seem to point to Billy's insecurities, or whatever it was that made him unable to separate himself from the organization. But that doesn't make Duke's manipulations any more noble. It was what it was, and I don't see anything wrong with telling the whole story. Both Duke's and Billy's music stand on their own, and their collaboration was one of the most brilliant, unique, and fruitful in the history of any music. But 2015 is Billy's centennial, and it appears we as a musical society still have some educating to do.[85]

The historical inaccuracies about the Ellington–Strayhorn collaboration tend to be perpetuated by some, not all, members of a very zealous Ellington fan base.

AFTERWORD:
CHERISH THE LEGACY

BY GREGORY A. MORRIS

As a youngster, I spent the first eight years of my life in one of the homes that Billy lived in before he moved to New York. My grandmother, who was Billy's mother, and my mother, who was the older of his two sisters, told me stories about how I would crawl under Uncle Bill's upright piano to play with the pedals and then try to stand up, always managing to bump my head on the piano's undercarriage. Mama Strayhorn and my mother used to tell me that Uncle Bill often worried about me hurting myself even though it seemed that I had a hard head. Uncle Bill would hug me and rub my head and whisper his special name for me. My sister Cheryll reminded me that our mother always talked about Uncle Bill using his first check from Duke Ellington to buy me a pair of shoes.

As the years passed, Uncle Bill did not return home very much, as his schedule became increasingly busy with his work with the Duke Ellington Orchestra. When he did come home, it was a great time of celebration for the family. On one of his trips to Pittsburgh, we talked about my high school experience and discovered that my English teacher at Taylor Allderdice High School was the same teacher he had had as a high school student at Westinghouse High School. From that time on, he always asked about her, and I usually had a message from her to give to him whenever he would call.

Uncle Bill was a very giving person. He helped me make my first tuition payment to the University of Pittsburgh and proudly sent me money to pay my initiation fee for Omicron Delta Kappa, a national

Billy with his eldest nephew, Gregory A. Morris. In 1964 Billy asked him to "take care of my stuff" as executor of his estate.

leadership honor society. The year 1955 was very special for my cousin Carole and me. We were the most recent Strayhorn family high school graduates, and Uncle Bill wanted to do something special for us: he planned an all-expenses-paid, weeklong trip to visit him in New York City.

We saw the sights, met his friends, and met such celebrities as Dodgers baseball stars Roy Campanella and Jackie Robinson, championship boxer Sugar Ray Robinson, and popular vocalists Lena Horne, Billy Eckstine, and Nat King Cole. He even took us to lunch at Lena Horne's home. We attended the Broadway play *Silk Stockings*, spent a day at Coney Island amusement park riding the Cyclone roller coaster, checked out a performance at the Apollo Theater, and explored the heights of the Empire State Building. As we walked the streets of New York, people would stop to talk to Uncle Bill, and he proudly introduced his niece and nephew. When asked, Uncle Bill said this was his first time visiting Coney Island and the Empire State Building, and he was having a great time.

Billy with his nuclear family in a photograph by brother John (kneeling in front) at a family gathering in the early 1950s. From left: Lillian Young Strayhorn (mother), James Jr., Billy, Lillian, Georgia, Theodore, and James (father).

The best was yet to come, however, because Uncle Bill also had work to do. The Ellington orchestra was scheduled to perform at the Aquacade Auditorium. We went backstage to meet Mr. Ellington and then enjoyed the performance from front-row seats. At intermission, we had to say good-bye to Mr. Ellington, who had another engagement. We were saddened for a moment until we returned to our seats for the second half of the show. Much to our delight, Uncle Bill walked out on the stage, bowed to the audience, and began to conduct the Ellington orchestra for the remainder of the show. This was truly a "wow!" experience for me because I had never seen or heard the Ellington orchestra play with Uncle Bill as the conductor and pianist!

Uncle Bill enjoyed and encouraged his nieces and nephews. My brother Michael remembers Uncle Bill giving him money to buy a trumpet he had seen in a pawnshop. My cousin Leslie remembers talking to Uncle Bill about all kinds of music and musicians. Once, she specifically asked him about the Beatles, who had just come on the scene, and he said, "They are damn fine musicians, and good music is good music." My sister Alyce remembers inviting Uncle Bill to come hear her high school chorus. Uncle Bill went with her on the "A" train to get there. As she introduced him to teachers and classmates, she was surprised that they knew who he was. My sister Cheryll recalls that every time she left Uncle Bill in the hospital, he always asked her for a Hershey bar. Cheryll also shared that Uncle Bill sent her, Alyce, and Leslie to see Ella Fitzgerald, and to their good fortune, Duke Ellington introduced them to her.

From reading *Lush Life*, Uncle Bill's biography written by David Hajdu, it seems that in the late '50s and early '60s, Duke Ellington was becoming more involved with theatrical/musical productions such as *Saturday Laughter* and *Jump for Joy*. These shows were not well received by many audiences, perhaps because they were beyond what many had come to expect of Ellington music. The film version of the outstanding novel *Anatomy of a Murder* was thought to be an even greater stretch. Ellington took on these immense projects but soon turned over the responsibility of arranging and producing the final versions to Uncle Bill.

This effort consumed a major part of Uncle Bill's time, but it turned out to be worthwhile. After the filming and recording of the soundtrack for the film *Paris Blues*, record producer Alan Douglas, who was very involved with the *Paris Blues* project, spoke with Uncle Bill about a special recording session. The outcome of this session was an album titled *The Peaceful Side*. Many scholars, friends, and longtime Strayhorn followers viewed this effort as Strayhorn finally playing his music as he intended it to be played.

Uncle Bill loved fine clothes and good food and drink. He loved to entertain in his apartment. He and his friends went to museums, Broadway shows, and clubs

Family members gather outside Westinghouse High School to celebrate the 1995 placement of a Pennsylvania historical marker honoring Billy Strayhorn. He is also pictured in the WHS Wall of Fame with fellow musical alums Linton and Erroll Garner, Nelson Harrison, Art Nance, and Mary Lou Williams.

around town. As a teenager in Pittsburgh, he read the *New Yorker*, so as an adult living in New York, he wanted to do everything he had read about. Uncle Bill had many friends who were dancers, and he joined their club, the Copasetics, in 1949 when it was founded. He served as the club's president from 1951 until his death in 1967. In honor of Uncle Bill, the Copasetics abolished the position of president after he died.

In the early '60s, Uncle Bill sensed that his health was becoming an issue. Tobacco and alcohol were

Billy's extended family posed at Ellington '95: The Thirteenth Annual International Conference on the Life and Music of Duke Ellington. The event was dedicated to Billy's memory and hosted by the Billy Strayhorn Chapter of the Duke Ellington Society. Delegates from thirty-four states and sixteen countries attended.

not his allies. In the early '60s, Uncle Bill asked me if I would be the executor of his estate. I said yes but also inquired what he wanted me to do in that position. His answer was strong and specific: "Take care of my stuff!" He said this while pointing to the numerous books and multiple folders of music materials in his small apartment. That was to be my task. Uncle Bill had his will drawn up on July 30, 1965, naming me as his executor. His mother died in October 1966, and he followed her seven months later on May 31, 1967.

The responsibility for the Billy Strayhorn estate fell to me. I met with Uncle Bill's attorney to determine what my next moves would be. I had to ask myself such questions as, *What do I have to do to take charge? What do I need to identify and safeguard, as any of his possessions could have great meaning to his family and perhaps even the future generation of musicians? What belongings might make up Uncle Bill's legacy?*

His was a small apartment, but it was bursting with the book collection of an avid reader; issues of *DownBeat*, the *New Yorker*, *Time*, *Life*, *Look*, and *Saturday Evening Post*; daily newspapers; and music scores/sheet music. Uncle Bill had beautiful ashtrays, vases, and artwork purchased from his world travels, as well as a small television, a Grundig tape recorder, reel-to-reel tapes, a turntable, speakers, and records of all sizes. He had several paintings from Paris, plus a wooden elephant and some metal containers from India. He also had a four-drawer cream lateral file cabinet, where he kept his folded clothing. Before he died, he gave his Steinway piano to St. Peter's Lutheran Church on Lexington Avenue at Fifty-Fourth Street in New York City, where it currently stands. Uncle Bill gave the piano to St. Peter's because of his friendship with Pastor John Garcia Gensel, who was known for his "jazz ministry."

Because Uncle Bill had no wife or children, the court determined that the executor would have the right to make all decisions about his property, including his music. This included decisions regarding copyrighting, renewing copyrights, and terminating rights to use his music. One major task I had was determining the value of his financial holdings, including royalty income for his music and his outstanding debts and liabilities. Working through this task took considerable time, talent, and resources. I had to find and hire independent attorneys to represent the interests of the estate.

Uncle Bill died in the first twenty-eight-year term of the copyrights held by particular publishers, so it was assumed that the agreements made in the first term would continue for the second term. As the executor of the estate, I challenged that assumption in court. The court ruled that I, as the executor, could enter into new copyright agreements for the second twenty-eight-year term. Additionally, the Sonny Bono Copyright Term Extension Act of 1998 gave me the opportunity to terminate the previous agreement to enter into a copyright term extension. In response,

FROM TOP: In fall of 1963 Billy traveled with the Ellington orchestra on a lengthy tour of the Middle East and India under the auspices of the US State Department. Ellington fell ill almost immediately upon arrival in India—Billy led the group in Duke's absence. Billy bought this carved elephant home as a memento of the trip. § Billy bought these metal boxes in India and kept them for himself. In one he placed a lock of hair from his beloved mother, Lillian.

The 1968 Grammy awarded posthumously to Strayhorn and Ellington honoring their thirty-year collaboration and creation of "many great sounds sweet and hot, warm and cool."

recording of some newly discovered pieces. He also published a book on Billy Strayhorn's music called *Something to Live For: The Music of Billy Strayhorn*. As a result of Walter's work, our family copyrighted over seventy songs.

As Uncle Bill's musical works became more widely known, some of his heirs started getting deluged with requests to make his music available to a younger and broader audience. Thus, in 1997, our family created a formal organization called Billy Strayhorn Songs, Inc. (BSSI) so that we could meet the requests of scholars, musicians, and others who were interested in Uncle Bill's work. To make Uncle Bill's music available, BSSI has worked with a number of major publishers throughout the world. We hope that this centennial celebration will continue BSSI's mission to create a greater appreciation for all of the music that Billy Strayhorn produced during his fifty-one years of life.

the publisher holding the second twenty-eight-year term agreement took us to court, arguing that the twenty-year extension belonged to the publisher. The court again ruled in my favor as the executor.[86] Under the copyright term extension, we became copublishers with DreamWorks.

After David Hajdu completed his biography of Uncle Bill, *Lush Life*, in 1996, he received a visit from Walter van de Leur. Walter was a visiting musicologist from the Netherlands who asked David why he kept seeing the name Billy Strayhorn in connection with Duke Ellington while he was studying Ellington's music at the Smithsonian Institution. Walter later contacted me to examine some of Uncle Bill's music that I had acquired. Several visits to Pittsburgh and a close examination of the materials in the Strayhorn collection led Walter to return to Pittsburgh to study, play, and eventually record previously unknown works. Walter's work later evolved into a dissertation and the

ABOUT BILLY STRAYHORN SONGS, INC.

Thirty years after Billy Strayhorn's death in 1967, his family established Billy Strayhorn Songs, Inc. to bring recognition to the composer and his significant contributions to the world of music. The goals of the new company were to make Strayhorn's music available to the public and to capture, manage, preserve, and expand the artist's legacy.

Today, BSSI continues to achieve these goals by managing and monitoring the production, sale, and distribution of Billy Strayhorn Manuscript Editions charts and scores, and by granting the rights to use Strayhorn's music in live productions. BSSI also works with several other publishers to administer the Strayhorn catalog, and it is involved with such groups as the International Association for Jazz Education and the Jazz Education Network. BSSI is also partners with the Music Institute of Chicago and the Esther

Boyer College of Music and Dance at Temple University, each of which offers a Billy Strayhorn scholarship for jazz music.

In 2011, BSSI established the Billy Strayhorn Foundation, Inc. to help perpetuate the Strayhorn legacy by celebrating his life and his music. The nonprofit BSF works to develop a deep and widespread appreciation for Strayhorn and jazz music in general through live music performances, lectures, and symposiums. In celebration of the centennial year 2015, the BSF created the Billy Strayhorn Centennial Committee to plan events aimed at exploring and expanding Strayhorn's musical legacy.

Since it was established in 1997, BSSI has worked to see that the image and legacy of Billy Strayhorn continue to move "ever up and onward," as was Strayhorn's motto. The twenty-first century already has seen several acknowledgments of the greatness of Strayhorn's music. A *Time* magazine poll cited "Take the 'A' Train" on its list of the one hundred top songs of the twentieth century. The June 2001 edition of *Ebony* magazine listed three Strayhorn compositions on its list of the twentieth century's one hundred best songs by black composers. The December 1999 edition of *Pittsburgh* magazine named Billy as one of its one hundred most influential Pittsburghers of the twentieth century.

The Strayhorn name is often inextricably linked to Ellington's when fans refer to the music of Ellington/Strayhorn, but Strayhorn is coming into greater recognition on its own merits, largely due to the work of BSSI. Looking ahead, the future looks very promising for BSSI as new media and new promoters offer fresh and exciting opportunities for Strayhorn's music to gain more exposure. BSSI's work is far from over, as it is always looking for new ways to continue managing and sharing the Strayhorn legacy for generations to come.

ACKNOWLEDGMENTS

Billy Strayhorn Songs, Inc. would like to thank the many people and organizations who contributed to the creation of this book as well as who help to cherish and maintain the legacy of Billy Strayhorn:

Lisa Alter, Esq., who as our attorney provided legal guidance in shepherding Billy Strayhorn Songs, Inc. (BSSI) from its beginnings. Herb Jordan, Esq., the first manager for BSSI. Past and present BSSI board members who have contributed their skills in law, education, business, and the arts to establish BSSI and to develop a model that will enable successors to perpetuate the legacy of Billy Strayhorn: specifically, Gregory A. Morris, PhD, executor of the Strayhorn estate and founding president of BSSI; Lawrence C. Strayhorn, past president; and Leslie M. Demus, Esq., founding president of the Billy Strayhorn Foundation.

Thanks to everyone who provided insight and contributions to this project through their interviews and to David Hajdu, Robert Levi, and Walter van de Leur, PhD, for their seminal works that have enlarged the understanding of the Strayhorn legacy and for their contributions to this project. Much appreciation is owed to Bruce Mayhall Rastrelli, DMA, for his research and writing on Strayhorn's civil rights legacy. Additional thanks to Bruce for researching the images of this book and for writing their captions. Thanks to Reservoir Media as copublisher of the Strayhorn catalog and to Agate Publishing.

BSSI would also like to acknowledge the various people and organizations who helped contribute images and memorabilia for this project, including the Carnegie Museum of Art, the National Museum of American History, the Smithsonian Institution, the Logan family, David Hajdu, Robert Levi, Fred Kenderson, the Orange County Historical Museum, the Joe Alper Photo Collection, Barbara Wright-Pryor, Joan Watson-Jones, Hermene Hartman, and Jane Goldberg's Changing Times Tap Dancing Co.

Thanks to Ellington–Strayhorn devotee David Hill for his permission to use his thoughtful insight. And thanks to Ramsey Lewis for contributing his reflections in the foreword.

And endless thanks to all those fans, musicians, and teachers who continue to perpetuate the music of Billy Strayhorn.

NOTES

1   This essay is an amalgamation of family stories and remembered conversations with my uncle Billy Strayhorn, informed by the works of David Hajdu, Robert Levi, and Walter van de Leur as well as tête-à-têtes with jazz aficionados in my capacity as a producer of jazz programs and my involvement with jazz education.

2   Barry Ulanov, *Duke Ellington* (New York: Creative Age Press, Inc., 1946), 219.

3   Robert Levi, *Independent Lens*, "Billy Strayhorn: Lush Life," *Independent Lens* video, 1:23:41, February 1, 2007, http://vimeo.com/98073796.

4   They both studied music education at the University of Pittsburgh and became the first and second black teachers in the Pittsburgh Public Schools system. Judge Homer S. Brown, for whose election Nelson worked, permitted her to select five of her students from the NAACP Youth Council to become the first black women to teach in the district.

5   Her nephew, Nelson Harrison, wrote me May 13, 2014: "She always told me how gracious Billy was to her during those years." Both Nelson girls grew to be brilliant educators and strong voices for civil rights in their adulthood.

6   Dr. Sophia Phillips Nelson, quoted in the *New Pittsburgh Courier*, 13 April 2011.

7   In 2011 Dr. Nelson won posthumous recognition of her sister's honor from Westinghouse High School, Pittsburgh Public Schools, the city of Pittsburgh, and the legislature of Pennsylvania. Fannetta died in 2008.

8   Sophia was contributing reporter for the *Pittsburgh Courier* series "*What's What in Our High Schools*" describing the outstanding activities of WHS minority students. In her article of December 26, 1931, she wrote: "The Penn Club of Westinghouse High School consists of only eight members. Two of these, William Strayhorn and James Randolph, are colored. The members were chosen by the sponsor because of their ability to write essays, compositions and short stories. The members also take part in various literary contests."

9   David Hajdu, *Lush Life: A Biography of Billy Strayhorn* (New York: North Point Press. Farrar, Straus, Giroux, 1996), 15.

10 "Interest Keen for 'Penthouse Party'," the *Pittsburgh Courier*, August 17, 1935. http://www.newspapers.com/image/40231617/?terms=Strayhorn+scholarship

11 *Pittsburgh Press*, April 25, 1937; Hajdu, *Lush Life*, 30.

12 High school clarinetist friend Jerome Eisner, cited in Hajdu, *Lush Life*, 39.

13 Lena Horne and Richard Schickle, *Lena* (Garden City, NY: Doubleday and Company, Inc., 1965), 99–100.

14 Ibid., 42.

15 Ibid., 45.

16 *The Crisis*, May 1939, 86.

17 *Journal of the National Medical Association*, May 1974; 66(3): 272–273.

18 Vivian Perlis and Libby Van Cleve, eds., *Composers' Voices from Ives to Ellington: An Oral History of American Music* (New Haven: Yale University Press, 2005), 408.

19 Ibid., 404.

20 Walter van de Leur, *Something to Live For* (New York: Oxford University Press, 2002), 283–284 and 268.

21 See a description of these non-sleepovers and Billy's use of the term in Hajdu, *Lush Life*, 196.

22 Ibid.

23 Description of the Logans' home from their son, Warren Arthur "Chip" Logan, in conversation with the author, December 3, 2014.

24 Tracy Sugarman, *Drawing Conclusions: An Artist Discovers His America* (Syracuse, New York: Syracuse University Press, 2007), 58–63 passim.

25 Gail Lumet Buckley, *The Hornes: An American Family* (New York: Alfred A. Knopf, 1986), 185.

26 Ibid., 247.

27 Ibid.

28 NAACP, "Excerpts from Remarks by Miss Lena Horne," June 7, 1963; NAACP Records, LOC, Group III, Box E-9, Folder 8, in Michael Vinson Wiliams, *Medgar Evers: Mississippi Martyr* (Fayetteville: University of Arkansas Press, 2011) Kindle location 6150.

29 Ruby Hurley, NAACP Southeast regional secretary, testified that Beckwith was one of the three. See "Seek End to Jackson Injunction," *The Crisis* (March 1964), 182. Hajdu provides the detail of the request that the men not smoke while Lena was singing, *Lush Life*, 227.

30 Horne and Schickle, *Lena*, 285–286.

31 His activities are recorded in Ken Vail, *Duke's Diary, Part 2* (Cambridge, England: 2002), 220–223; *Ellington Sessions* http://www.depanorama.net/63.htm and *The Duke Ellington Chronicle or The Duke—Where and When: Duke Ellington's Working Life and Travels.* http://ellingtonweb.ca/Hostedpages/TDWAW /removed20131124-nextTDWAWPartTwo.html#Yr1963

32 Terry Teachout, *Duke: A Life of Duke Ellington*, (New York: Gotham Books, 2013), 316.

33 Stuart Nicholson, *Reminiscing in Tempo: A Portrait of Duke Ellington* (Boston: Northern University Press, 1999), 346.

34 Harvey G. Cohen, *Duke Ellington's America* (Chicago and London: University of Chicago Press, 2010), 392.

35 Edward Kennedy Ellington, *Music Is My Mistress* (Garden City, NY: Doubleday and Company, Inc., 1973), 198.

36 Nicholson, *Reminiscing in Tempo*, 346.

37 Ibid., 228.

38 Hajdu provides this detail of scheduling (*Lush Life*, 230). Newspaper coverage in the *New York Amsterdam News* and the *Pittsburgh Courier* both give the previously scheduled later date.

39 Ibid., 229.

40 Marshall and Jean Stearns, *Jazz Dance: The Story of American Vernacular Dance* (New York: Macmillan Publishing Company, 1968, Da Capo Press edition, 1994), 262.

41 Stearns, *Jazz Dance*, 261. Copasetics Honi Coles and Cholly Atkins were "interviewed about a thousand times for their book," see Cholly Atkins and Jaqui Malone, *Class Act: The Jazz Life of Choreographer Cholly Atkins* (New York: Columbia University Press, 2001), 138.

42 Copasetics 1963 program. Generously provided by Andrew Nemr, cofounder, taplegacy.org.

43 Cohen, *Duke Ellington's America*, 394.

44 Alyce Claerbaut, personal conversation with the author, November 18, 2014.

45 Hajdu, *Lush Life*, 229.

46 Ibid, 235.

47 Ferdinand Jones, "Eloquent Anonymity," *Readings: A Journal of Reviews and Commentary in Mental Health* (March 1997), 13.

48 Joe Mosbrook, "Cleveland Jazz History, Second Edition" (2003), *Scholarship Collection*. Book 135, 43. http:// engagedscholarship.csuohio.edu/scholbks/135

49 Hajdu, *Lush Life*, 20.

50 Images from the Hajdu Collection: Library of Congress presentation copies, © 1934.

51 Van de Leur suggested the possibility of Wood's authorship of the melody and Billy's harmonization in *Something to Live For*, 8, though I take it a step farther.

52 Mosbrook, "Cleveland Jazz History," 43.

53 Hajdu, *Lush Life*, 67.

54 Ibid., 66–67. In an email to the author on October 21, 2014, Hajdu revealed: "I promised one living person not to mention in the book that he and Strayhorn were lovers. That was Haywood Williams." Williams died in 2002.

55 *Independent Lens*, "Billy Strayhorn: Lush Life."

56 Hajdu, *Lush Life*, 174.

57 Atkins and Malone, *Class Act*, 93.

58 Hajdu, *Lush Life*, 119.

59 Ibid., 171–172.

60 Ibid., 201.

61 The *New York Times* (1 December 1991), Obituary.

62 1914–1955. His middle name was W (not an initial). His birth certificate may be accessed at ancestry.com.

63 Carol J. Oja, "Sailor from On the Town, Dunham Dancer, and Visual Artist: Frank Neal" in *Bernstein Meets Broadway: Collaborative Art in a Time of War* (New York: Oxford University Press, 2014) is an excellent source. Margaret Goss Burroughs recollection, "Chicago's South Side Community Art Center" provides additional information about Neal's activities in Chicago: http://iwa.bradley.edu/ChicagoCommunityArtCenter.

64 U. S. Census, 1940. Thompson was treasurer of Defender Publications in Chicago (*Chicago Defender*, May 21, 1955).

65 His first Broadway casting, in *Carmen Jones*, opened on December 2, 1943; the show ran until February 10, 1945. He was regularly engaged as a dancer through 1951 in *On the Town*, 28 December 1944 to 2 February 1946; *Finian's Rainbow*, 10 January 1947 to 2 October 1948 (dance captain). See *Internet Broadway Database*, http://www.ibdb.com/person.php?id=94816. He also danced in *Peter Pan* (the Bernstein version), 24 April 1950 to 27 January 1951 (listed at IBDB as "Fred" Neal) and its abbreviated national tour thereafter.

66 Oja, *Bernstein Meets Broadway*, 206 and Hajdu, *Lush Life*, 114, 115.

67 The Bloomsbury Group or Set was a group of English intellectuals in the first half of the twentieth century whose works "deeply influenced modern attitudes toward feminism, pacifism and sexuality." It included Virginia Woolf, E. M. Forster, Lytton Strachey, and John Maynard Keynes (among others). http://www.k-state. edu/english/westmank/literary/bloomsbury_resourc-es.html

68 Oja, *Bernstein Meets Broadway*, 205–206; Hajdu, *Lush Life*, 114- 115.

69 Hajdu, *Lush Life*, 115, 117.

70 Ibid., 247.

71 *Chicago Defender* (National edition, 21 May 1955); *New York Age* (May 14, 1955).

72 Hajdu, *Lush Life*, 194.

73 Ibid., 247–249, 251, 253–254 passim.

74 Adam Gopnik, "Two Bands: Duke Ellington, the Beatles, and the Mysteries of Modern Creativity," the *New Yorker*, December 23, 2013.

75 Alyce Claerbaut, conversation with the author, December 14, 2014.

76 *Jet*, 22 June 1967.

77 Hajdu, *Lush Life*, 116.

78 In spite of the legend, Billy said he did not sing "Lush Life" for Duke in 1938. At its public premiere at Ellington's Carnegie Hall concert of November 13, 1948, Duke introduced it as "a new tune." After Nat King Cole's recording on March 29, 1949, it became a major hit. Billy spoke at some length thereafter with Pat Harris, a writer for *DownBeat* magazine. He said, "*Lush Life* was not the first tune of mine Duke heard. In fact, he didn't hear it until just a little while ago. I wrote it in 1936 when I was clerking at the Pennfield drugstore on the corner of Washington and Penn in Pittsburgh." He continued with other interesting facts about the song's use in the years between 1936 and 1948. See "New Hit, 'Lush Life,' Is Not New," *DownBeat*, August 12, 1949.

79 Ibid., 18.

80 Teachout, *Duke: A Life*, 197.

81 David Hajdu, "A Jazz of Their Own," *Vanity Fair*, May 1999, pp. 188–196.

82 http://www.kalamu.com/bol/2006/06/25/john-coltrane-johnny-hartman-%E2%80%9Clush-life%E2%80%9D/

83 Hajdu, *Lush Life*, 79.

84 Personal conversation with the author, November 18, 2014.

85 David Hill, post on the Duke Ellington–LYM Listserve, 2014. Quoted with permission.

86 Music Sales Corp. v. Morris, 73 F. Supp.2d 364 (S.D. N.Y. 1999). http://www.leagle.com/decision/199943773FSup-p2d364_1390.xml/MUSIC%20SALES%20CORP.%20v.%20MORRIS

CONTRIBUTORS

A. Alyce Claerbaut holds a masters degree in education. After a career as a university administrator she left in 2002 to participate in the newly formed Billy Strayhorn Songs, Inc., a family-owned music publishing company. She presently holds the position of president, interacting with music publishers, producers, and educators on behalf of her uncle's legacy. She is musically trained with a concentration in voice, has performed professionally, and is an active jazz advocate and promoter. Ms. Claerbaut was named "Chicagoan of the Year" in Jazz in 2011 by the *Chicago Tribune*.

David Hajdu is the author of *Lush Life: A Biography of Billy Strayhorn*. The first book ever published about Strayhorn, *Lush Life* was the result of more than ten years of research. It was named one of the Hundred Best Nonfiction Books of All Time by the *New York Times* and won multiple honors, including the Deems Taylor Awards for music writing. Hajdu is a professor at Columbia University, the music critic for *The Nation*, and the author of three other books, all award winners.

Galen Demus, nephew of Billy Strayhorn, joined the board of directors for Billy Strayhorn Songs, Inc., in 2005. He has worked in jazz education, promoting the legacy of Billy Strayhorn though several music-centered initiatives, including starting the Billy Strayhorn Jazz Education Scholarship in 2008. He has played a pivotal role in coordinating the participation of BSSI and the Billy Strayhorn Foundation in the annual Jazz Education Network Conference, solidifying the musical and historical presence of Billy Strayhorn for an audience of students ranging from middle school through college, jazz educators, and professional musicians both in the United States and abroad.

Leslie M. Demus is heavily invested in community service. She is a former trustee of the New Rochelle Public Library and currently on the board of the New Rochelle Public Library Foundation. She contributes to the New Rochelle Public Library community on its board of trustees as well as by working as a fundraiser, spokesperson, and creative thinker to modernize technology, create quality programming, develop special projects, and ensure quality service for library patrons.

Ms. Demus serves on the board of Billy Strayhorn Songs, Inc. and also is president of the Billy Strayhorn Foundation. She spent almost twenty years in advertising and was a Vice President/Senior Attorney at Ogilvy & Mather Worldwide. She met her husband, Ralph C. Dawson, in law school. They have two sons.

Gregory A. Morris earned a PhD from the University of Pittsburgh before working as a teacher, supervisor, and administrator in Pittsburgh Public Schools from 1959 until 1993. After a short retirement, he joined the University of Pittsburgh's School of Education as an associate professor. After retiring again in 2005, he completed a teaching career of forty-five years. He remains active in numerous community service, cultural, and church organizations.

At the request of his uncle, William Thomas "Billy" Strayhorn, Gregory became the executor of his uncle's estate in 1967 and continues to serve in that capacity. He worked with his family members to create Billy Strayhorn Songs, Inc., in 1997. He became the corporation's first president and currently serves as board director at large.

Gregory is married to Thelma L. Morris and has three children.

Bruce Mayhall Rastrelli earned degrees in choral music, music history, and conducting. His forty-five-year career included university teaching and performance in academic, community, and professional settings. With Alan Broadbent and Joanna Gleason, he led the creative team that produced an all-Strayhorn concert in Los Angeles in 2007 and formed the curriculum of an innovative schools outreach program. He will direct a revival of this concert at Auditorium Theatre, Chicago, in celebration of the Strayhorn centennial.

Robert Levi is a writer, director, and cinematographer. In 2008, his film, *Billy Strayhorn: Lush Life*, became the first program in broadcast history to receive the Emmy for Best Documentary, the Peabody, and the Writers Guild Award for Best Documentary Screenplay. The film was one of three documentaries included in *New York* magazine's Ten Best Television Programs list. His film *Duke Ellington: Reminiscing in Tempo* premiered on PBS's *American Experience*, and also received an Emmy. His recent film, *Playwright: From Page to Stage*, featured Robin Williams and premiered on PBS's *Independent Lens* series.

William E. Strayhorn attended Point Park College in Pittsburgh. In 1963, he began his career at the nuclear power station in Shippingport, Pennsylvania, where he worked primarily in contract administration relative to nuclear purchasing. In the mid-1990s, his career interests merged with his involvement in Billy Strayhorn Songs, Inc., where he has contributed vital support to clearly define emerging contractual issues. Since 2009, he has acted as vice president of the board.

John C. Strayhorn attended the University of Pittsburgh where he earned bachelor of science in psychology and master of arts in education. He has been employed with the Goodyear Tire and Rubber Company for more than thirty-two years where he has held numerous positions throughout his tenure with Goodyear's North American Operations.

Strayhorn has served on the board of directors of Billy Strayhorn Songs, Inc. for more than five years and currently serves as treasurer.

Walter van de Leur is a jazz musicologist who received his PhD for his research on Billy Strayhorn, published as *Something to Live For: The Music of Billy Strayhorn* (Oxford University Press). He conducted extensive research at the Smithsonian's Duke Ellington Collection and researched and catalogued Billy Strayhorn's personal files in the possession of his estate. With the Dutch Jazz Orchestra he recorded four CDs including rediscovered works by Strayhorn (Challenge Records). Van de Leur teaches at the Conservatorium van Amsterdam and is a professor of jazz and improvised music at the University of Amsterdam.

ILLUSTRATION CREDITS

Each credit line includes the photographer, when known, and the collection where the image resides. If more than one credit is provided for a page, images are listed clockwise from top left and separated by a semicolon. If only one credit is provided for a page with multiple illustrations, the credit applies to every image on the page. Reproductions of all music manuscripts are © 2015 Billy Strayhorn Songs, Inc.

PHOTOGRAPHER AND INSTITUTION ABBREVIATIONS

BSSIC   Billy Strayhorn Songs, Inc. Collection

BWP   Courtesy of Barbara Wright-Pryor Williams

CH   Charles "Teenie" Harris, Photograph © 2015 Carnegie Museum of Art, Pittsburgh

CVV   Library of Congress, Prints & Photographs Division, Carl Van Vechten Collection, LC-USZ62-114529

DB   Photograph by Dunc Butler

DEC   Archives Center, National Museum of American History, Smithsonian Institution, Duke Ellington Collection, 301, Series 7

DHC   David Hajdu Collection

DS   Duncan P. Schiedt Photograph Collection, Archives Center, National Museum of American History, Smithsonian Institution

EW   Painting by Eddie West

FDC   Frank Driggs Collection, Archives Center, National Museum of American History, Smithsonian Institution

FK   Photograph by Fred Kenderson

GA   Photo by Gordon Anderson

JA   Photograph by Joe Alper courtesy of the Joe Alper Photo Collection LLC

JGA   Jane Goldberg's Changing Times Tap Dancing Co., Inc. Archive

JM   Photograph by John Miner

JWJC   Joan Watson-Jones (née Carrington) Collection

LFA   Logan Family Archive

MB   Photograph by Marc Beloeuvre

NAACP   Library of Congress, Prints & Photographs Division, Visual Materials from the NAACP Records, LC-USZ62-84478

OCHM   Orange County Historical Museum, Hillsborough, N.C.

RLC   Robert Levi Collection

U   Photographer Unknown

WG   William P. Gottlieb/Ira and Leonore S. Gershwin Fund Collection, Music Division, Library of Congress

vi: DB DHC **viii**: U RLC **x**: RLC **3**: BSSIC **4**: BSSIC; RLC **5**: DHC **6**: DHC **8**: DHC **10**: U BSSIC **12**: DHC **13**: BSSIC **14**: OCHM **15**: BSSIC **16**: BSSIC **17**: U **19**: DHC **20**: DHC **21**: DHC **22**: DHC **23**: DHC **24**: DHC **25**: DHC **27**: U DHC **28**: U DHC **30**: RLC **31**: BSSIC **34**: BSSIC **36**: RLC **37**: DS **38**: BSSIC **39**: BSSIC **40**: JA; U DEC **42**: FDC **43**: BSSIC **45**: U BSSIC **46**: BSSIC **47**: DHC **50**: BSSIC **51**: BSSIC **52**: BSSIC **53**: FK BSSIC **54**: DB DHC **55**: LFA **56**: DHC **57**: BSSIC **58**: GA DHC **59**: DHC **61**: CH **62**: DB DHC **63**: BSSIC **64**: JM DS **66**: DHC **69**: CH **70**: U DHC **72**: U BSSIC **73**: WG **74**: U DHC **75**: BSSIC **77**: LFA **78**: CVV **79**: BSSIC **80**: WG **82**: U DHC **83**: U DHC **84**: LFA **86**: U DHC; BSSIC **89**: U DHC **90**: DHC **92**: U DHC **93**: BSSIC **95**: LFA **96**: LFA **97**: LFA **98**: NAACP **100**: LFA **101**: LFA **103**: CH **105**: LFA **106**: LFA **107**: LFA **108**: LFA **109**: LFA **110**: U DHC **113**: U RLC **114**: BSSIC **116**: LFA **119**: CH **120**: BWP **121**: U DHC **122**: BSSIC **124**: EW JGA **126**: U DHC **128**: CH **129**: CH **132**: DS **133**: DHC **134**: U DHC **135**: U DHC **136**: U DHC **139**: U DHC **140**: U BSSIC **141**: U DHC **142**: LFA **144**: U DHC **147**: DS **148**: LFA **149**: BSSIC **152**: U DHC **154**: LFA **155**: LFA **156**: LFA; DHC **157**: LFA **159**: JWJC; LFA **161**: DS **162**: U DHC **165**: U DHC; MB DHC **167**: CH **170**: JM DS **171**: WG **173**: DS **174**: U DHC **176**: U DHC **178**: BSSIC **179**: BSSIC **180**: BSSIC **181**: BSSIC **182**: BSSIC **183**: BSSIC **189**: GA DHC **Front cover**: U RLC **Back cover**: U DHC

INDEX

Italic page numbers indicate photographs or reproductions of scores. An italic *t* following page numbers indicates an entry in the timeline. Bold page numbers indicate major discussions of a composition.